WHERE IS GOD?

Peter Fransen's answer to that question is bold and inspiring: God is here, in everyday life, in man himself. This presence of God is His grace and is "sown like a seed in the depth of the soul."

For centuries, Christians have debated the nature of grace. As the argument grew heated, it became more and more technical. The reality of God's love was hidden behind a mountain of abstractions.

In this book, which first took shape in the form of discussions with lay men and women, a renowned theologian cuts through the jargon and, making use of modern psychology, shows how grace works in each of us—not only in saints but in sinners and the mentally ill.

"It would be difficult to find a better introduction to the theology of grace, or a better explanation of its reality."

—*The Way*

Other MENTOR-OMEGA Books of Interest

Divine Grace and Man

PETER FRANSEN, S. J.

Revised Edition

TRANSLATED FROM THE FLEMISH
by GEORGES DUPONT, S.J.

A MENTOR-OMEGA BOOK

Published by
THE NEW AMERICAN LIBRARY

This book was first published in 1959 under the Flemish title *Gods
Genade en de Mens,* by Uitgeverij Patmos Antwerp

Nihil obstat:
John A. Goodwine, J.C.D.
Censor Librorum

Imprimatur:
✠ Francis Cardinal Spellman
Archbishop of New York
December 5, 1964

The nihil obstat and imprimatur are official declarations that a book or pam-
phlet is free of doctrinal or moral error. No implication is contained therein that
those who have granted the nihil obstat and imprimatur agree with the con-
tents, opinions or statements expressed.

Library of Congress Catalog Card Number: 61-15719

MENTOR TRADEMARK REG. U.S. PAT. OFF. AND FOREIGN COUNTRIES
REGISTERED TRADEMARK—MARCA REGISTRADA
HECHO EN CHICAGO, U.S.A.

MENTOR-OMEGA BOOKS are published *in the United States* by
The New American Library of World Literature, Inc.,
501 Madison Avenue, New York, New York 10022,
in Canada by The New American Library of Canada Limited,
156 Front Street West, Toronto 1, Ontario,
in the United Kingdom by The New English Library Limited,
Barnard's Inn, Holborn, London, E.C. 1, England

PRINTED IN THE UNITED STATES OF AMERICA

Foreword

During the year 1954, I had occasion to lecture on some of the ideas in this book at the Circle for the Study of Man, founded at Antwerp, and still run by Professor René Dellaert of the Catholic University of Louvain, Belgium. Teachers and youth leaders urged me to work out a number of other subjects proposed for discussion, first, at the Commission Internationale du Plein Air held in 1955 at Freiburg im Breisgau, and later at the Paris Commission Catholique des Colonies de Vacances of 1956, presided over by His Excellency Bishop René-Joseph Piérard. The year after, I had an equally sympathetic audience at the Grail House in Edinburgh, Scotland. These successive discussions led me on to write a more technical article for the international review of religious education, Lumen Vitae (*Brussels*), "Towards a Psychology of Divine Grace." [1]

Friends wanted a Flemish translation of this article. They were of the opinion that the work, rewritten in less technical terminology, would greatly interest a wide Flemish and Dutch public, increasingly mindful of religious problems.

The present slender volume is published from a motive of deep gratitude toward the Catholic laymen in Flanders whom

[1] English ed., XII, 203-232; reprinted in William Birmingham and Joseph E. Cunneen, eds., *Cross Currents of Psychiatry and Catholic Morality* (New York: Pantheon, 1964), pp. 31-61.

I had the privilege of meeting at numerous religious study circles in towns big and small.

A theologian, or a priest, could hardly envision a more enviable task than making the glories of the faith known. The attention, at once fervent and recollected, of so many of my countrymen as they listened to me was most rewarding. In the face of the longing for religious knowledge evidenced today in so many lay circles, silence is no longer permissible. Besides, it is a tradition in our country that theologians— for instance, Blessed Jan van Ruysbroeck—do not confine themselves to the pursuit of pure knowledge, but feel a responsibility toward God's people, the souls consecrated to Him in baptism and confirmation. Let us add: the lessons a theologian learns from such contacts with the laity cannot be overrated.

In gratitude and homage, then, I dedicate this little work to the adult Catholics of my country. To them we owe the fact that, in recent years, the preaching of the word of God has been lifted out of the rut of routine and formalism, and that sermons and religious instruction ring once more with something of the Eu-aggelion, *the* Good Tidings.

Note to the Second Edition

In this new edition we have some alterations in the wording and style of the text. Passages that seemed obscure or apt to be misunderstood have been carefully rewritten.

We thought it useful to add a few additional sections to Part II of the book in order to acquaint the reader better with some of the most important aspects of the doctrine of grace. The numerous quotations from the works of Blessed Jan van Ruysbroeck are designed to keep the present writing in line with the rich tradition of our national past.

Surprise has been expressed in some quarters at the length of Part I, dealing with the nature of theology, which certain reviewers say is not warranted by the title of the book. But they fail to perceive that these sections serve as the foundation of what comes later. My conviction remains unshaken that we shall not succeed in imparting anything like an *adult* faith to the laity by merely presenting them with one or another "new" insight. They should be shown how and why our doctrine is inseparable from a deeper insight into the methods proper to religious thought. We do not expect the laity to content themselves with repeating what we tell them; rather, we want them to grasp the way new conceptions have come about. "Be ready always with an answer to everyone who asks a reason for the hope that is in you," wrote St. Peter to his flock (I Pt. 3:15).

Contents

Introduction

This book on grace has been written not without serious apprehension. It is a formidable assignment to provide within the limits of a slender volume all that is necessary for an adequate, clear insight into one of the most central and most debated tracts of our Christian belief. Students of theology attend lectures on it for a whole year, four times a week; and usually they do not succeed in touching on all the aspects of this rich and intricate subject. Writing a book on grace is not made easier for an author when he realizes that many of the prospective readers are unfamiliar with theological methods.

Viewed from God's side, grace signifies, before all else, the wealth and majesty of God's love. Enfolding mankind as a whole, this love also embraces each single human being, as he is in his innermost nature and in his own peculiar situation in life. Grace, seen from God's side, signifies the sheer reality of the Blessed Trinity: Father, Son and Holy Spirit. It means our eternal election by the Father, the cardinal historical fact of the redemption by the Son dying on the cross and rising on Easter Sunday, the Lord's enduring presence in our history till the last day, through the power of the Holy Spirit—a presence coming to us through the Church, the sacraments and the preaching of the word of the Gospel.

Viewed from man's side, grace signifies rebirth in Christ. It denotes a mysterious but nonetheless eminently real stream of life which wells up from the deepest stratum of our being where it rests securely in the creative hand of God, up through all the slowly developing stages of our personality, irrigating and permeating the innumerable areas of our complex psychology, yet never ceasing to be a divine life, a purely gratuitous gift, God's constantly renewed and freely bestowed love. In the language of the Greek Fathers and the Byzantine theologians, grace is a new light which, on the day of our baptism, rises like dawn on the dim, remote horizon of our personal self, and in the soft morning glow of life dispels by slow degrees the darkness of sin and weakness—all this in preparation for and as a pledge of the midday splendor of a radiant eternity.

Every portion of our being has to be regenerated by grace: spirit and person, intellect and will, all our spiritual powers, from the psychic ego with its own peculiar temperament and character down to the lower psychosomatic regions of our animal bodily life with its obscure drives, its countless determinisms, its unconscious or semiconscious reactions. All these have to be reborn through grace.

Grace unites God and man. More exactly, grace is God's way of meeting man whom He came in search of and found lost in the solitude of an earthly sinful nature. In this meeting, God's love takes to itself man as he is, the whole of him, and makes of him a child of the Father, with and in the only begotten Son, through the power of the Holy Spirit.

Grace is the marvelous point of contact between two worlds: the world of the triune infinitude, and that of the utter nothingness which is man.

Notwithstanding its inherent difficulties, writing this book has cheered the author. He felt he was working for the Christian lay people who, of their own accord, have begun to demand a deeper understanding of their religion. The striking motto of a Lutheran lay movement in northern Germany, "The laity ask questions in their Church!" is indicative that our educated men and women look increasingly for an answer to the pressing questions of our times. Throughout the country, in places small and large, people are bestirring themselves, seeking an enlightened faith. Shall we at long last witness the end of that irritating, smug, inert and conventional Catholic life which carefully avoids religious problems, dodges the subtler queries of conscience, satisfies itself with a set of religious practices (euphemistically called "blind faith") and resorts to the excitement of mass demonstrations to make up for the absence of a convinced Christian policy? The new movement toward a more enlightened practice of the faith is only beginning; it resembles the hushed fleeting breath of early spring. . . . May it grow, go forward with the inevitableness of a phenomenon of nature. Better, may it bring about a thorough awakening in the Spirit.

The time has come to put a stop to a critical situation threatening the faith. The educated classes take it for granted that general culture and professional knowledge and skill keep pace with man's growth in responsibility toward the state and human society. Should a Christian not realize that he must outgrow the immature religious knowledge and practice of his high school and college days? The men and the women of our country should be possessed of the same dash and daring, the same eagerness for study, work and responsibility as are shown by those of other nations.

A lack of balance between secular culture and religious knowledge might be condoned, perhaps, in periods of quiet and peace, when traditional customs rule uncontested. In times of stress and strain, however, when many old ways of life are breaking down and new ones are still unformed, the interior tension between an underdeveloped religious consciousness and a fully developed professional competence can only raise doubts and dismay in the hearts of good Christians and bitterness and defection among the lukewarm.

It is by no means easy for an adult to approach matters of faith with an unprejudiced mind. Mathematicians, doctors, scientists, psychologists, lawyers and politicians unconsciously tend to bring to their study of religion the trusted canons of their respective specialities. They reflect on religion—and "do theology"—in the light of scientific methods, or from a political angle, or in conformity with the formal precision of a jurist.

Theology is a science like other sciences. Like them, it has its own proper object and is governed by its own special laws and methods. To these theology must hold fast if it is to be true to itself.

These introductory remarks will justify the divisions of our book:

I. What is theology and what are its methods?

II. What is grace?—or the application of theological methods to our subject matter.

III. What should man expect from grace?—or glimpses into some important points of contact between the theology of grace and the secular human sciences.

What

Part I

Is Theology?

Anyone familiar with the history of the sciences will know that our modern sciences began their triumphal march into Western culture on the day they broke loose from Greek, Arabic and Scholastic philosophy, struck their own path and followed their own laws. To cite one instance, medicine hovered for centuries among natural philosophy, black art and common sense, as long as the doctor cared more for Aristotle's four elements than for the etiology of the sickness he had to cure. Or again, astronomy, notwithstanding remarkable discoveries by Chinese, Chaldean, Egyptian, Phoenician and Arabic observers, hesitated among astrology, poetic fantasy and mathematical precision as long as it was preoccupied with theology, natural philosophy and the Bible, or with fate rather than the patient, systematic investigation of facts. In those days, it was often the case as with the famous logician who said, *"C'est logique, donc c'est vrai. Tant pis pour les faits!"* ("It is logical, and therefore true! Hang the facts!")

The cultured man of today is justified in protesting when views that have nothing to do with strictly medical research (as, for instance, the rigid lines of Marxist orthodoxy) are imposed upon men of science. Only foolish, untutored minds will want, on sentimental or nationalist grounds, to tamper with or garble well-established medical experience. It is no fault of the doctor if he happens upon antipathetic microbes.

17

The Special Nature and Method of Theology

We have grown rather sensitive, in some ways perhaps too sensitive, on the question of the autonomy of the sciences. This is often the case when a scientific attitude has become so aggressive that it demands for the sciences an unrestricted autonomy and then also investigates theology and philosophy. Catholics themselves are not always prepared to acknowledge that medicine, in both theory and practice, may have to take into account higher claims, such as those of moral theology and conscience.

It is perfectly correct to decry attempts to interfere with the legitimately autonomous exercise of human thought and power in their rightful spheres; but then, we should be ready to respect the claims of theology in its own sphere.

It is a joy to see how present-day laymen warm to religious problems. And the joy is genuine. But it makes one shudder to hear what some of them have to say in conversation, or to read what is printed in articles, books or book reviews—as was the case not so long ago after the publication of Giovanni Papini's famous book on Satan. On such occasions, one receives the impression that, in some sections of society, encouraging a personal study of religious doctrine gives a signal for a free-for-all fight. Sentiment takes the field; fancy and emotion come to the fore, but especially personal animosity against a self-important theologian, a somewhat assertive parish priest or religious with naive views of God and His designs. These dispositions do not make for a sound frame of mind or fruitful religious study; nor would they in other fields of learning. Such ill-conceived displays of sentiment need not cause undue alarm, but Rome has more than once thought it wise to raise a warning voice against an irresponsible spirit of destructiveness and anarchy.

It is quite normal that intelligent laymen, acutely aware of the needs of the time, should want to deny the monopoly of religious study to Scholastic theologians who show themselves overconfident perhaps in their monastic or clerical speciality and are in the habit of knitting their brows whenever a layman ventures upon a fresh theological idea. Difficulties do not come from the side of the laity only. I remember the sour remarks of a curate at the close of a meeting for religious study: he could not stomach that lay people should be served with three arguments in favor of a theological thesis when he himself had been given only one at the seminary.

This sort of thing happens in all domains of knowledge. Each rising generation is out to secure recognition for certain data of experience and finds itself at odds with its predecessors in the fields, whether these be great scholars, retired now and resting on their laurels, or less famous disciples. It is not the object of science that is at stake but certain particular positions and defective, outdated methods. Why, one may ask, would this not apply to matters theological? Why frown on every and all attempts to renew theology, to make it intelligible to the present generation, to look for answers adapted to our times rather than hold on to solutions suitable to the twelfth and thirteenth centuries? It should not be forgotten, though, that a fruit tree is rejuvenated by pruning and grafting, not by wholesale uprooting. A misguided zeal may lose sight of this danger.

Some words may be quoted here from John Henry Cardinal Newman, one of the first men of our age to realize the need for a laity thoroughly grounded in religious matters: "I want a laity, not arrogant, not rash in speech, not disputatious; but men who know their religion, who enter into it, who know just where they stand, who know what they believe and what they do not, who know their creed so well that they can give an account of it, who know so much of history that they can defend it. I want an intelligent, well-instructed laity." [1]

Theology and the Method of the Positive Sciences

Theology forms a branch of learning that in some respects has much in common with the positive sciences. The latter

[1] *Lectures on the Present Position of Catholics in England* (Dublin: Duffy, 3rd ed., 1857), p. 360.

always start, consciously and methodically, from carefully chosen experimental phenomena. The facts of experience are marshaled and interpreted in the light of their orderly recurrence. Their laws are established, classified in ever-widening hypotheses and worked out into increasingly comprehensive syntheses; but contact with the facts is never lost. New data and more accurate experimentation, suggested by the already discovered laws and hypotheses, are designed to extend those same laws, to improve upon them and shade them in their constant interactions. Whoever neglects the facts indulges not in science but in fantasy.

Theology proceeds in very much the same way, but along its own lines. Its basic object is not so much a body of truths, a determined doctrine or system, or even a definite philosophy of life; it is first and foremost the fundamental fact that *God has spoken to man in history*.

Whether it is studied according to the strictly scientific lines of professional theology or after the fashion of the life-centered theology of the lay groups, it will always be Revelation that provides the subject matter for consideration. Revelation, God's word spoken to man, is also the primordial and dominant fact of salvation. We are told so in the solemn opening verses of the Epistle to the Hebrews: "God, having spoken of old to our forefathers through the prophets, by many degrees and in many ways, has at last in these days spoken to us by his Son, whom he has appointed heir of all things, and through whom he made the world" (Heb 1:1-2). God speaking to man is thus a historical fact: the Son of God has become man, has spoken, has acted in the fullness of His being and with the consciousness of His mission and power. We are told this by the same Epistle to the Hebrews in the immediately following lines: "[He,] being the effulgence of God's glory and the very image of his substance, upholds the universe by God's powerful mandate" (Heb. 1:3). Theology is thus essentially bound up with the facts of Revelation.

The wealth of the divine reality and its truths were revealed to man in the historical person of Jesus Christ, and entrusted to His Bride, the Church, as an inalienable, intangible, undiminishable, incorruptible treasure. Part of her experience of Christ the Church has set down in a certain number of historical documents, called Holy Scripture. These documents or books were written under the inspiration of the Holy Spirit; the truths they contain are therefore guaranteed by the same Holy Spirit. It follows that in Holy Scripture we possess the written word of God, an incomparable, ever-new font of Christian faith and life.

While writing these sentences, I recall with grim humor the remark of a man present at one of our theological study meetings: "But why do you always deal with Paul, John and Mark? I should rather hear something taken from a modern author!" That good man failed to see that his religion is a revealed one, and that, surpassing the testimony of even our best modern thinkers, God's word in Holy Writ is an irreplaceable source of faith, of light and of living strength; it is a charter we are bound to follow in our theological investigation and study.

Scripture and Tradition

We hold then that Holy Scripture forms the basis of our faith, but not Scripture alone. Though written, as we said, under the special inspiration of the Holy Spirit, Scripture came into being as the first witnessing of the apostolic Church as well. The Church of the Apostles played a unique role in the historical course of Revelation. She stood under the guidance of the Twelve, those pre-eminently authentic witnesses of Christ's life, death and resurrection and of the mysterious descent of the Holy Spirit. Further, the primitive Church was herself privileged to hear the Lord in person, to listen to His preaching and to watch His works, and she was the first to believe through the power of the Holy Spirit. To her Christ spoke; to her, His Bride, He revealed Himself. She it was who, in the persons of the Apostles and the first disciples, could contemplate the Lord on the cross, touch the sacred wounds in the risen body, and hear the words of farewell: "And behold, I am with you all days, even until the consummation of the world" (Mt. 28:20).

All this is ample evidence that the Church existed before Holy Scripture. No one can deny that the sacred books owe to divine inspiration their exceptionally important role of being the authentic source of the faith; and yet we have to admit that they are at the same time neither more nor less than the divinely inspired expression of the apostolic Church witnessing to the faith. In them, the primitive Church uttered her belief for the first time; she set down in human language her experience of Christ; she meditated on it all. We discover in Scripture the first beginnings of a true theology, coming as such under the immediate guidance of the Holy Spirit.

That is why Catholics consider Tradition to be the source of their faith. Tradition, well understood, is not just a number of unwritten truths still held today by the Church. Tradition is that which is handed on by the entire life of the Church in Christ through the power of the Holy Spirit: her liturgical prayer, her sacramental actions, her dogmatic pronouncements in matters of faith and morals by general or provincial councils, her ordinary daily preaching of the faith as proposed always and everywhere by the teaching authority of the bishops united under the primacy of the Roman pontiff.

Tradition and Scripture cannot be separated from each other. Right at the beginning, Tradition gave rise to the written word, which has in return nursed and guided it ever since. To speak of two different sources of faith would be unfortunate. The matter is quite simple, really: Tradition and Scripture, keeping true to their respective natures, enrich one another by their mutual relations within the Church; both are the voice of the Church speaking to us in the name of God.

In both Tradition and Scripture, God speaks to us through the Church, though not in the same manner. Scripture is inspired by the Holy Spirit; it communicates to us, for instance in the writings of Paul, Peter and John, the very words of God in their most pregnant meaning. In her Tradition, the Church receives only the "assistance" of the Holy Spirit. The technical term *assistance* means simply that in her primitive tenets and aspirations, in her authentic life of faith and morals, in her universal unanimity through time and space and in her papal or conciliar pronouncements, the Church cannot falsify, cannot distort or mutilate the treasure of Christian Revelation.

The distinction between Scripture and Tradition is deeper than a mere difference of technical terms. Holy Scripture belongs to the period of Revelation proper, to the "fullness of time"; it is the authentic word of God heard in apostolic days; it remains always part of the historical reality of Revelation—together with the primitive Tradition, of course. From the moment this privileged period was closed, ecclesiastical Tradition has been entrusted with the one task of *keeping intact* the primordial treasure of Revelation, or, in the words of Paul, "the deposit of faith." It preserves it, however, not as a lifeless thing, a dead letter without spirit, but as a living truth which, remaining ever itself, unfolds, clarifies and enriches itself.

Understood in this sense, the living Church in her living Tradition constitutes a second source of theological thought.

These are the facts from which all sound religious investigation must start if it wants to stay true to itself and avoid heterodoxy. Heterodoxy is human speculation to which the spirit of the age may lend charm and appeal, but which retains too little of what is absolute, immutable and divine in God's own word.

Thus, the facts are these: first, the fundamental fact of Christ, the Word of God in human gesture and speech; and then, through Christ and the Spirit, the fact of the Church, of her Scripture and Tradition.

Because of all this, the prime attitude of the Christian, desirous of applying himself to the study of God's word, should be one of religious attentiveness and reverent contemplation as he listens not to a man but to God whenever He speaks to us in the Church. To give some instances, Christ has died to redeem us, and we needed to be redeemed because we were born estranged from God and lost. These are facts we read of in Scripture. That Christ is true God and true man is also a fact proposed to us by Scripture and by the infallible Ecumenical Council of Chalcedon. It is another fact, defined by the Councils of Florence and Trent, that there are seven sacraments. Again, it is a fact, attested by the unanimous and absolutely unerring Tradition of the Church, that children must be baptized. It is still another fact, held by the Church from time immemorial and therefore ages before Pius XII defined it on November 1, 1950, that the Blessed Virgin Mary was assumed body and soul into heaven.

Let us observe here in passing that the pope, notwithstanding his supreme teaching authority, prepared the dogma of the Assumption only after consulting with the faithful scattered throughout the universal Church. No one, not even the pope, can act by his own authority and apart from the living faith of the entire Church. The intangible treasure of the faith has been given to the Church as a whole. Paul wrote to the Galatians who had been led astray by the intrigues of a few fanatical Judaeo-Christians from Jerusalem:

I marvel that you are so quickly deserting him who called you to the grace of Christ, changing to another gospel; which is not another gospel, except in this respect that there are some who trouble you, and wish to pervert the gospel of Christ. But even if we, or an angel from heaven, should preach a gospel to you other than that which we have preached to you, let him be anathema! As we have said before, so now I say again: If anyone preach a gospel to you other than that which you have received, let him be anathema! [Gal. 1:6-9]

Not Paul, nor John, nor any ecumenical council, nor bishops in their capacity of teaching body and successors of the Apostles, nor the pope himself can preach a Gospel other than the one kept alive by the virtue of the Holy Spirit in the everlasting Church.

Virtually, it is all but one voice, one vast chorus of ages and peoples—the voice of the Church which neither may nor can behave otherwise than as the herald of the Father through Christ, in the power of the Holy Spirit.

In that powerful choir the Father has spoken His transcendent Word; all theology must start from that Word. Whoever overlooks this, whether deliberately or in sheer ignorance, is no theologian, no student of religion, but just a religious dreamer. Whether he is guilty or not matters little; he is a dangerous man because theology (like other domains, such as medicine) deals with questions of life and death. Its concern is God and His sacred Word, Jesus Christ; it is all or nothing.

Theology, an Investigation

When all the facts relevant to a given religious theme (like grace, for instance) have been ascertained, the second task of theological thought begins. With docility, the mind has now to ponder the facts supplied by faith; it has to seek an insight into them, to try to get a synthesized grasp of their meaning, content, relations and unity.

They have, of course, but one meaning only, one that is solidly based on the fundamental structural unity of God's word. God's word, manifested both in Revelation and in the redemption, is necessarily one, like Himself. It takes root in the inscrutable depth of the initiative of the one Father; it grows through the creating, redeeming Word of the one Son; it is given cohesion and lasting perfection through the silent action of the one Spirit—all this within the precincts of the one Church, God's temple on earth. God does not act as we do; He does not hesitate, grope His way, with fresh starts every now and then. From His very first Word in creating till the last consummating word at the end of time, God proceeds in one act, with one thought, one plan of salvation. This unity of the divine operation gives each of the many truths and realities of faith its organic place in the whole, and thus also its ultimate meaning. The intent and purpose of theology rests on this basic fact.

Religious study for laymen has the same intent. It should start on its way with all the reverence due to God and His word; it should persevere with childlike trust in the unity of God's loving action, and so come to realize the ultimate meaning and full import of all that God has done and said in the Church. Obscurities are bound to remain as long as we are on earth. God has not deemed it necessary for our salvation that all questions should be solved. However, when reflection goes hand in hand with prayer and investigation with faith, the unique magnificence of the divine redemptive action, surrounding us on all sides, cannot fail to dawn upon us by degrees and to warn us of the meaning of life—our own and that of our loved ones. We shall see that we come from God and return to God, in order that, believing, we "may have life, and have it more abundantly" (Jn. 10:10).

Unity and Diversity of the Sciences Concerning Man

We have dwelt at some length on the similarities between theology and the other sciences about man. We now point to a few basic differences. We cannot think of seeing them all,

or of treating them in all their aspects. We shall have to restrict ourselves to a few practical remarks, enough to make
possible an exchange of views with the sciences that study
man from other angles. Such an exchange is not only reason-
able but necessary. Man is a living whole; he asks questions
about himself, and wants to be accounted for in his totality.
He objects to being itemized and dissected "scientifically,"
inasmuch as the conclusions of one science seem to con-
tradict those of another. I am a living being, one reality to
myself. I have a right to unity of truth concerning myself,
notwithstanding the unavoidable specializations of biochem-
istry, psychology, sociology and philosophy. This wish grows
more and more articulate in the face of the excessive specialization to which the study of man is exposed. The sciences
of nature are making rapid progress toward a satisfying, integrated body of knowledge. Why not the same in the science
of man? Theology deals with man, man seen from God's
point of view; it cannot neglect the deep-seated need for a
unified knowledge.

But let us not simplify matters to excess. Unified knowledge is not to be had merely by scraping together some ill-
assorted conclusions from various sciences. Truth is both
one and many-sided—just as man is. It must be built up
organically, with due regard to the many facets and possibilities of expression belonging to the richly varied life
which is ours.

Moreover, each science possesses a specialized method imposed on it by its own particular subject matter, and this
method traces out the limits within which the given science
sets to work. A psychology of man which claimed to swallow
up all other knowledge of man would fail to keep true to itself and would destroy itself. One is never sufficiently on
one's guard against the totalitarian tendency so characteristic
of all forms of specialization. Specialists make so much of
their own technique and achievements that they soon find
themselves unable or unwilling to accept the fact that there
are other aspects beyond the scope of their methods.

In this connection, we would call attention to a great difference between the experimental sciences and philosophy.
The former increase the number and precision of their tests
in order to secure a more comprehensive understanding of
their respective area of human experience, while philosophy
makes straight for what is absolute in our being. Now, theology may be compared to the natural sciences insofar as

it endeavors to describe accurately the data bearing on salvation and contained in Revelation, but theology is more akin to philosophy as regards its nature and degree of certitude; it seeks to reach what is absolute and eternal in the divine plan concerning us in Christ and the Spirit.

We do not have the space or the occasion to go into the problem of the oneness of human thought taken as a whole, or to consider it in its full range and complexity. But one important point needs singling out here: the words at our disposal for an exchange of views with the other sciences about man must be used correctly.

The Correct Use of Words

It is surprising to notice how much human thinking is dependent on the spoken or written word, on vocabulary and grammar. Some philosophical lines of thought cannot thrive in certain countries because the literary humus, the idiom of the people, is unfit for such speculation.

Be that as it may, man cannot think accurately without the help of a precise terminology. Every language is limited in its vocabulary, so much so that one and the same word may possess widely different meanings, arising from very unexpected causes. To give one example, the word *tank* signifies, of course, a large receptacle for storing liquids; but it may also mean "a type of armored car running on caterpillar wheels, equipped with a crew and guns, for attacking an enemy in difficult country." The latter meaning happens to have been introduced by the British in December, 1915, for the purpose of secrecy during manufacture.

As regards language, theology faces a rather hopeless task. Like any other science, it borrows its words where it can, from everyday life or from the other sciences, especially philosophy. These words strike their deepest roots in the primitive subsoil of a definite culture; worse still, however spiritualized they may have grown to be by now, they are words belonging to earth. Unavoidably, they are influenced by the historical development that every nation and linguistic region must undergo. Rationalism is badly mistaken when it asserts that words and their connotations are completely independent of the evolutionary process of the culture to which they belong. Few things are as interesting as the history of a single word, and nothing is more delicate. Words and their meanings may be compared to the modulation of a voice: one can tell the primary tone from the overtones or harmonics to which the voice owes its richness, its warmth and charm.

A word possesses a basic meaning which evolves appreciably in the course of time. It is the product of a particular cultural milieu with its own individual temperament and its own peculiar set of problems in the general human climate. In such circumstances, a word cannot help adding to its original basic sense numerous varying resonances not always recorded within the covers of a dictionary. Much research and *esprit de finesse* are needed to recapture the rich scale of tones a word has acquired through the centuries. For example, the word *democracy* means different things for men in the United States, England, the Benelux countries, France and the Marxist regions. Among Asians and Africans, its meaning is often unknown. Man does not think with his reason only; he thinks with the background of his whole being, his time and race. To stand by reason exclusively would produce unrealistic and inhuman illusion. Actual experience bears out the truth of Shakespeare's lines, "What's in a name? That which we call a rose/ By any other name would smell as sweet." Nothing is so fleeting and illusive as a word.

And it is with words that theology must endeavor to speak to man of the absolute, the unchangeable, the eternal —of God and His work of salvation.

Theological words, in their mold of sound and script, must do duty as symbols not of human experience and knowledge but of the transcendent divine truth. They have to translate for us not what we think or experience but what *God Himself says and thinks of us*. No man in his right senses would have ventured to take such inadequate material to express God's message if God Himself had not set us the example in Holy Scripture and especially in His Son. The Son of God, the eternal Word of the Father, did not hesitate to speak to mankind about His Father, about His own person and about the divine plan in the language of uncultured Galilean fishermen and peasants. The Church does now what the Son of God did in Palestine. She is all the more justified in doing so in matters for which she comes under the guidance of the Holy Spirit.

In theology, words do not entirely escape their human fate. Our times have made the discovery that even theology has gone through a development. To illustrate this point, let us follow one or two case histories. It is clear now that the term *revelation*, apart from its primary meaning derived from Scripture, connoted "assonances" in the Middle Ages which it no longer possesses today. To the medieval mind, *revelation* spontaneously raised the question of private revelations: what was their nature and what were the obligations they entailed? Today, after the *Aufklärung* with its inquiry into the natural revelation of God in creation, and after the First Vatican Council, we understand *revelation* to mean almost exclusively the eternal truths which God manifested, not through creation but supernaturally. Some theological textbooks may still have a word to say on the subject of private revelations; they do so, however, out of fidelity to the old Scholastic way of proceeding. Modern trends have changed; spontaneous reactions are different.

The same remarks apply to the term *faith*, in the sense of content of faith and dogma. Until and even during the Council of Trent, the term had a much broader meaning. Then it did not spontaneously suggest truths immediately revealed by God and proposed as such by the Church, as it has since the seventeenth century and, more definitely, since the First Vatican Council. The problem presented itself rather differently. In the framework of earlier Scholastic theology, the word *faith* pointed above all to the criteriological properties of our supernatural knowledge. Faith is both obscure and certain. In the eyes of the medieval theologian, its obscurity linked it with opinion, while its absolute certainty allied it with *scientia* or deductive knowledge. It seemed also to belong to the moral plane of obedience to the Church. *Faith*, consequently, stood for whatever the Church could infallibly propose and impose as necessary means toward eternal salvation; thus, it also stood for the truths which could be deduced with logical certitude from the truths of faith, and even for the universal ecclesiastical laws. These last two we would no longer call "truths of faith." Things have not changed objectively, but vocabulary and psychological outlook have taken on a different perspective.

All this explains why great efforts are being made today to recover the original and exact meaning of the words used in Scripture. Patient research has resulted in the production of detailed dictionaries for both the Old and the New Testament. What is more, it has shown the need to try to recapture the philosophy or mentality hidden in the vocabulary. We have come to realize more clearly than ever the obvious principle of the *Imitation: "Omnis Scriptura debet legi eo spiritu quo scripta est"* ("Texts of Scripture must be read in the spirit in which they have been written"). For a whole century, exegetes have had to do battle against the rationalistic bias of theologians in order to reconquer what is theirs by right. We are perhaps not yet technically equipped for a critical study of ancient conciliar texts, but everything points to the evident necessity of it. As the French proverb has it, *"Donnez-moi la parole de quelqu'un, et je le fais pendre"* ("Give me anyone's words, and I will hang him on them"). Taken out of the context, any word can be forced to fit any desired sense; deftly handled, the words of Scripture itself can be twisted into rank heresy.

It would be naive to suggest that this view of human thinking smacks of Modernism. True Modernism sinks all certitude concerning God in the shifting sands of human search and speech, stops there and looks no further. All thought, every spoken or written word is fatally caught in the perpetual flux of an ever-varying stream of human history.

Even from a purely human standpoint, this view is false. Though we speak in different tongues and think in different climates, we are nonetheless able to understand each other through the ages and everywhere—clear proof that we speak of the same common experiences, the same basic truths and realities of life, though in different words and perspectives.

The Modernist view is in a worse state still when we consider the Church. When Christ promised her His Spirit, He did so with the purpose of ensuring that the living, growing truths entrusted to her would develop in perfect fidelity to themselves. And here an important point should be made. The infallibility with which Christ has endowed His Church includes the right of attaching a definite truth to a definite word. It is quite possible that, as Karl Barth and others assert, the notion of *person* has evolved so much that in its modern usage the word no longer expresses aptly the mystery of three Persons in one God. However, the Church did choose the word *person* to designate each one of the three centers of divine life in the Trinity. She uses it in her councils, her liturgy and her catechism. As a society of men, she is entitled like any other human society to select, or to coin if need be, those words which seem to her most suitable for expressing her authentic teaching. Furthermore, the Church is also a divine institution, thus enjoying an enhanced right to connect the trinitarian truth with a definite terminology. In case the men of today—at least, those who belong to some philosophical or phenomenological school—stand in danger of misunderstanding one or another term, it would be the part of the theologians to explain it to them and to enlighten them concerning the true mind of the Church.

All things considered, there is not the slightest reason for changing the term *person*; so many words in our Western vocabulary possess different meanings. Besides, the Church's fidelity to ancient traditional expressions, in spite of linguistic evolution, has a higher significance: it underlines the intangible nature of her inheritance, the faith. Nothing prevents her from meditating more deeply on the riches of the mystery contained in the formulas consecrated by Tradition. But to meditate on the truths of faith does not mean to go back on and rectify earlier thought. What the Church does is to deepen her grasp of it and to declare more explicitly what she has always been aware of, though with less precision perhaps, in the past.

That is the way the Church guards the treasure she inherited, the deposit of faith; but she may not allow it to mummify. Faith remains an ever-living truth—on the condition only that it does not renounce itself. Fidelity to the primordial data of Revelation, combined with a growing understanding of "what is the breadth and length and height and depth" of the divine mysteries, is the exclusive privilege of the Church as a divine-human society. If she was not endowed with Christ's own teaching power and with the abiding assistance of the Spirit, the Church, like any other human society, would be apt to corrupt and deform her initial inspiration and intuition—a process which Toynbee has described in a masterly way.

It is fitting, then, to stress how fortunate it is for ecclesiastical language to be independent of evolutionary changes in culture, though it stays within the flux of time. Like a living organism, the Church takes into account the varying developments of language and schools of thought, but she keeps faithful to herself and to her Lord.

Need we repeat now that this way of conceiving evolution differs radically from Modernism? Modernism in essence consists in the persuasion that religious expression—and that includes dogma—can be nothing but an indefinitely changing representation of both the momentary religious experiences and the collective religious perceptions at a given point of history. It amounts to pure relativism, therefore—the subtle temptation of our age.

From what precedes comes the evident conclusion that in our religious study we may not forget the exact meaning of our words. This obligation increases when we enter into discussion with educated persons, men of science, let us say, who obviously have an accurately defined vocabulary of their own.

To take an example bearing on the subject matter of this book, it seems impossible to speak of grace without mentioning sin, for grace brings with it deliverance from and remission of sin. Now, the word *sin* occurs in connection with other matters not belonging to theology. To a psychiatrist, it stands for a vague sense of guilt arising from either an inborn or an acquired anxiety complex. It indicates a depressing tension between different psychic tendencies and repressions which have not been adequately integrated into an interior equilibrium. Frequently, neither morality nor personal responsibility are involved, rather to the contrary: many psychiatrists tend to emphasize its impersonal and nonvoluntary aspects. Anxiety can grow into a cancer causing disorder, or disquiet and dissatisfaction, or it may turn into an oppressive anxiety fixation, and yet never reach the personal depth where religious sin is rooted.

The philosopher, on his side, thinks of sin along other lines. To him, sin means infidelity to self, a want of existential authenticity in respect of self, a deliberate strengthening of a fundamental urge in nature and eventually also a freely accepted offense against the absolute rule of all morality, or, finally and at best, a preference given to self away from or against the absolute source of all being and action.

For the theologian, there can be no question of sin except at the spiritual level where the free "commitment to life" takes place; and in this, the theologian is at one with the philosopher. But seen from the standpoint of Revelation, sin is a great deal more than that: it is a revolt against the living God. More explicitly, it is self-sufficiency turning away in proud self-love from God's all-enveloping love; it is a sacrilegious refusal to be and to live with Christ as child of the Father.

It has been rightly remarked that the depth and the godlessness of sin, as mentioned by Revelation, can be fathomed only in the measure that one progresses in the knowledge and love of God. That is why the saints and the mystics are the only ones to realize keenly the heinousness of sin, much to the discomfiture of our own hard-heartedness and earthbound dispositions. Sin, in the meaning it has in Revelation, is to be measured from God's point of view, from that of the divine wrath and abhorrence so starkly manifested by the sacrifice of the cross. Christ died on the cross to let us "sense," in a human, tangible manner, how utterly the All-Pure and the All-Holy condemns sin. The cross stands as the vivid symbol and disclosure of both God's wrath and God's love.

To express three rather divergent groups of facts, we dispose of only one word: *sin*. When a psychiatrist, a philosopher and a theologian meet to discuss the subject of sin, they land in the most senseless misunderstandings as soon as they forget that each one speaks of something different. Their purposes, too, are divergent. The psychiatrist does his utmost to relieve the sense of guilt in view of building up the patient's psychic equilibrium. One can understand that his speciality and the professional experience he has of a morbid religiosity in some of his clients may cause him to ignore the teaching of the Church about sin, or that he declares offhand the Christian notion of sin a menace to psychic health. We need not enter into this here.

The philosopher, looking at sin from a speculative point of view and taking his stand on general humanistic principles, may often see in it no more than the baneful, dark side of free will, the risk besetting all human existence. The theologian, on his side, bases himself on Revelation to stress the need of a sense of sin which, to the Christian mind, differs in kind from psychic anxiety. All the saints, outside periods of spiritual trial, have found great peace and strength in the sense of sin. A correct estimate of sin belongs to the essence of a genuine Christian faith.

The difficulty grows when we realize that these three qualitatively different realities meet together in the living unit of the same individual man and influence each other. On this score, the three approaches to the notion of sin differ among themselves, though they are nevertheless related to each other. The philosopher concerns himself with analyzing the structure of man's nature and the capacity to sin as such. Both structure and capacity work themselves out, in their

respective ways, in the fact of personal religious sin. And
because religious sin is essentially a spiritual lie, it reacts
generally on the psychic self in the form of a remorseful
sense of guilt. In the case of a psychologically unbalanced
individual or even of a man who is normal but unwilling
to rid himself of his sin, remorse may sometimes spread
like a leprosy and eventually impair psychic health. In any
event, there exists a relation between the psychic sense of
guilt and real sin against God.

Oratorical preachers rarely fail to make an impression
when they graphically enlarge on the death of a sinner.
Led by a deep-seated sensibility, priests and faithful tend
to forecast agonizing despair at the deathbed of any great
sinner. Events do not always turn out as anticipated. The
French writer Georges Bernanos, in his profound drama
Dialogue des Carmélites, has put on the stage the harrowing agony of the saintly prioress Mother Henriette du Nom
de Jésus. If we want something more striking, did the
All-Holy not lie prostrate in the Garden of Olives, crushed
by anguish and mental torture? On the other hand, we are
not unaware that many men, after an apparently evil life,
have met with a peaceful end. Psychic anxiety does not
necessarily go together with spiritual wickedness and guilt.
The nature of the sickness from which the patients suffer
may cause agony in some and euphoric hope in others till
the final end.

But let no one misunderstand me. It is not at all my intention to maintain that sinners, especially at the last moment, are generally free from remorse. All I want to suggest
is that sin and anguish, peace and innocence are not in-
variably linked together in actual life. Final impenitence and
obdurate revolt against God may very well leave something
like Satanic serenity on the face of a dead man.

What has been said concerning the word and the notion
of *sin* applies to other terms and notions. For instance, we
should know what we are talking about when we speak of
grace, particularly of the aspect of grace that we experience,
which is interior peace of soul. Mental peace means nothing more to the psychiatrist than an integrated equilibrium
of all the psychic powers working in healthy harmony. To
the philosopher, it stands for the conscious glow of well-
being which a man experiences when he commits himself
to his concrete, actual task in life with complete sincerity
and truth. The Christian, on his side, sees in peace of mind

the inner realization of God's love for him, a peace which the Lord alone can give. Among the saints, some have lived, for a time at least, in the earthly paradise of a rarely achieved balance between the natural and the supernatural powers; others have carried the treasure of an ineffable mystical peace in the midst of an anxious spiritual turmoil amounting at times to mental imbalance.

The powers which rule our lives run their course along parallel lines, each one according to its own laws. Normally, though, they show a marked tendency to combine into a mutually attuned rhythm of development. We find a remarkable illustration of this in the life of Theresa of Avila. The Protestant Walter Nigg, a well-known church historian, devotes some moving pages of his book *Great Saints* to the development of Theresa's harmonious growth in holiness. She spent twenty years in the Convent of the Incarnation at Avila, in the faithful observance of the approved rules and customs of that otherwise rather worldly cloister. Already then she was favored with the higher mystical states, and at the same time was disturbingly rent within herself, to the point of manifesting the strangest symptoms of sickness and catalepsy. It is foolhardy to try to unravel the secret working of grace in the saints. Nevertheless, Walter Nigg seems justified when he says that, at bottom, the cause of Theresa's illnesses lay in the deep-set conflict she experienced between her vocation to sanctity and the pull of some bourgeois or even worldly ways of life around her. No sooner did she surrender to the call of grace, in the spirit of the reformed Carmel, than another woman stood revealed in her, the greatest woman of her age. From then on she showed herself endowed with a firmness of character, a harmony of life, a quiet humor and an unrivaled spirit of enterprise which we quite fail to detect under the traits of her former semihysterical temperament. It is safe to suppose that in Theresa the complete victory of grace favored appreciably the robust psychological integration which we admire in the saint. Her irresistible feminine charm, her refined and yet childlike joy in life, her strength of character and power of organization, her stout and purposeful readiness to fight for the good cause—all these point not only to a heart totally reformed by grace but also to a human nature very nearly Edenic in its integrity.

Conclusion

And so we reach the end of the first part. We may sum up and conclude. If in our studies we want to hear what theology teaches, we shall have to accept and show becoming respect for the laws which rule it from within. We shall have to use words in the sense determined by theology, not by other sciences or branches of human knowledge. In case other sciences, also engaged in the study of man, make use of the same words, though with different meanings, we shall respect the notional difference and faithfully bear it in mind. Any other way of discussing religious problems produces nothing but confusion and stirs up endless difficulties that are absolutely uncalled for. Why jeopardize an earnest study of the faith by blurring the issues with a hopeless jumble of definitions of terms?

We shall inquire into the faith and take as our basis the rock-bottom facts of divine Revelation. The words we shall use cover realities not of this earth. They are but clumsy human means of designating the eternal designs which God Himself has deigned to reveal in and through the Church, Scripture and Tradition, but chiefly through His Son, our Lord, Jesus Christ.

We do not intend to proceed recklessly in the use of our words and definitions. And this for two reasons: firstly, because the realities they cover are organically interconnected in the unity of human experience; secondly, because in the complexity of life, those realities develop on their respective levels, each faithful to its particular pattern of laws and to its own individual purpose.

Part II   # What Is Grace?

When visiting an important museum, it is advisable to begin with an exploratory look through the principal halls. The theology of grace is a world by itself; what we have said in the first part of this book will help us find our way about in it. In order to set the problem in its proper light from the start, we shall avail ourselves of a parable. The rich symbolism of parables, tales or examples has the advantage of enlightening the mind to a surprising degree on one or another of God's secret dealings with man. Christ Himself had recourse to parables to teach the ineffable, to communicate to His hearers what had to remain hidden. Parables respect mysteries and speak to the whole man.

The Nature of Grace

A Parable

Once upon a time there was a young girl, an orphan, who grew up in coarse surroundings. Her foster parents were hard and rough, and had never wanted her. Never as a baby

or as a growing child had she known the subtle intimacy
of a true home. She had never been loved.

And then she grew into a young woman. Daily encounter
with disparagement, egotism and brutality hardened her
heart. All she knew was self-defense, daily surly bickering
to make sure of a minimum of security and right. To the
best of her knowledge, it had always been so in the past,
and it would remain so in the future: biting in order not
to be bitten—the law of the jungle. She had no faith in
man; she had not even faith in herself.

Her whole appearance betrayed the solitude in which the
soul of her youth was living. She toiled and moiled, dressed
in cheap, graceless attire. Her one means of escape from
hopeless emptiness was rough and rowdy amusement. Selfish,
suspicious and uncouth, with bitterness distorting her mouth,
she was aware that she had no beauty and that what men
wanted was her body for a few lustful moments.

There lived in the same city a young man, hale and
strong. His sunny youth, spent in the midst of loving parents,
brothers and sisters, shone in his gaze and sang in his
voice. His step and speech were assured and firm, as is the
case with those who have found peace. He was a good man.

One bright morning in spring, the miracle happened. The
young man met the girl by chance. Moved in his innermost
self, his heart went out to her. With the eyes of love, he
saw right through and beyond her shabby vulgarity. He
looked out for her; he spoke to her with the simplicity of
a conquered heart. But she laughed in his face at first, addressed him in crude, unmannered language. She thought he
was ridiculous.

But tact, patience and respect found their way at last
to a remnant of yearning which lay still unwithered in the
depth of the girl's being. For the first time in her life, she
was appreciated for her own sake—the greatest need of
human nature. Yet the beauty he discovered in her came
not from her but from his love.

Love has been a creative power since the beginning of the
world. The young man's deference and appreciation stirred
up in her a nascent self-reliance, a foretaste of peace and
quiet, of inner self-assurance. And timidly, gropingly, the
young woman awakened to first love. She shyly began taking
care of her appearance, though gaudily still and without
elegance. His tenderness and his example refined her taste.
Beauty came to her with the first smile.

Soon they became absorbed in each other. They steadily drew together in a selfless exchange of pure mutual love. What had happened really? Or better: what had come into being? That girl had been granted a great favor, a matchless present, a gift she did not deserve: the favor of love.

After the long, barren winter of her youth, a seed had been sown in her innermost self; it was ready to spring into life. Though still very much herself, she was already another person. She experienced a soothing security, welling up from unsuspected regions within her; she grew steadily in strength and depth, in proportion as her formerly cherished convictions were pulled up by the roots. It was like a painful dying. All the distrust, hatred and vindictiveness she had so far nursed in herself, whatever she had clung to with the despair of a drowning person, she had now to let go; she had to resign herself to the sensation of being stripped bare, bereaved of all. A harrowing agony, indeed, but one of which life is born.

Like a ship tossed on the waves and driven from her course, the girl tried another tack. She steered to the unknown: she made *the leap of faith in another*. The aggressive self-assertiveness, the armor in which she had shielded herself so far, was torn off her. She attempted *the leap of hope in another* who would in the future stand surety for her. Meanwhile, an unsuspected marvel happened: she felt enriched by her new state of bereavement, secure and anchored in her surrender. Faith and hope ripened into *real love*, the final leap, indispensable to anyone who wants both to lose himself and to find himself in another. The girl had lost everything she had, but what she lost she recovered superabundantly. She ceased putting her trust in appearances and now saw more deeply into things. She discovered the beauty of her surrounding world—the setting sun, the violet in the shade, the light in the eyes of a child, the laughter in a voice. She saw everything through the eyes of her beloved. She became another being altogether; for the first time, she was her true self. Her injured youth lived on in her, but it now began to develop along the lines of generosity and disinterested care of others—in a wealth of gratitude.

A beautiful tale, indeed. The one thing in it which leaves us somewhat skeptical is whether there ever was a young man powerful enough to work such a miracle. We read of the custom in honor among the conquistadores that when

they were caught in a storm at sea, they vowed marriage
with the first penniless girl God would put on their path
after a safe return home, with the proviso, naturally, that
the girl be sound of limb and morals. Whatever view one
takes of the parable or of the conquistadores' custom, it
is sure that only a very pure and powerful love can change
bitterness and hatred into a return of love. No mere man,
however, can achieve even that much, for wickedness is
rooted more deeply in our nature than we dare suspect.
That is why there had to appear a Man without sin, a Man
possessing God's own heart. And when He came, the tale
became reality.

God's Own Parable

Holy Writ speaks of that Man. Already in the Old Testament Yahweh tells the Jews, "Can a mother forget her
infant, be without pity on the child of her womb? Even
should she forget, I will never forget you. See upon the
palms of my hands, I have written your name; your walls
are ever before me" (Is. 49:15-16).

The parable of a moment ago we did not invent. It is
told in more gripping language by Ezechiel. The prophet
speaks, in Chapter 16, of the unique, undying love of God
for the faithless city, Jerusalem, which prefigures the whole
of mankind and the Church.

So saith the Lord God to Jerusalem! The land of thy origin
and birth is Chanaan; thy father was an Amorrhite, and thy
mother a Cethite [pagan lands turned away from God]. In
this manner wast thou born, in the day of thy nativity, thy
navel was not cut, neither wast thou washed clean with water,
nor rubbed with salt, nor wrapped in swaddling clothes. No
eye had pity on thee to do any of these things, out of compassion to thee; but thou wast cast out upon the open field,
because no one thought thy life worth while.

I, then, passed by thee and saw thee sprawling in thy
blood; and I said to thee when thou wast in thy blood:
Live. I bathed thee in water and washed the blood off thee,
and anointed thee with oil; I made thee look as fresh as the
flower of the field. And thou didst increase and grow great,
and advancedst, and camest to woman's ornament: thy

breasts were fashioned and thy hair grew; and yet thou wast naked and full of confusion.

And again I passed by thee and saw that the time of love had come to thee. I spread my garment over thee and covered thy ignominy. And I swore to thee and I entered into a covenant with thee, saith the Lord God; and thou becamest mine. And I clothed thee with embroidery and shod thee with violet colored shoes; and I girded thee about with fine linen, and clothed thee with garments of silk. And I decked thee also with ornaments and put bracelets on thy hands, and a chain about thy neck. . . . Thou wast made exceeding beautiful and wast advanced to be a queen. And thy renown went forth among the nations for thy beauty; for it was perfect through the luster I put upon thee, saith the Lord God.

But trusting in thy beauty, thou playedst the harlot because of thy renown; and thou hast prostituted thyself to every passerby to be his. . . . [Here the sacred author describes the "prostitution" of Jerusalem.] Thou didst also build thee a brothel. . . . Thou hast made thy beauty to be abominable; and thou hast prostituted thyself to every one that passed by, and hast multiplied thy fornications. [These "fornications" will bring Jerusalem to commit the most unnatural deeds.] Adulterous woman, thou hast brought strangers in the place of thy husband. Gifts are given to all harlots; but thou hast given hire to all thy lovers, and thou hast given them gifts to come to thee from every side to commit fornication with thee. [Ez. 16:3-33]

The significance of this gripping chapter, describing the eternal drama between God and man, will come home to us better when we realize that the term *prostitution*, used by the prophets especially in connection with the covenant, means the sin of idolatry. To commit "fornication" is to betray the covenant, to renounce and forsake Yahweh as the one true God, to reject His eternal love and to believe in false deities. As most of the cults practiced by Israel's neighboring peoples were mixed with religious prostitution and human sacrifice, the term *fornication* was a telling one to the Jewish mind. In Ezechiel's text, the literal and figurative senses overlap and mix, as in the casting away of children, the offering to the deities, the various allusions to the lewd practices among the people.

Israel's sin is more grievous than those of Sodom and Samaria. God will punish Jerusalem more than any other nation. In the punishment, however, lies also forgiveness, for God remains ever faithful to His first love. It is in this way that we should read and understand the conclusion of the chapter. "Thus saith the Lord God: I will deal with thee, as thou hast despised the oath in breaking the Covenant; and I will remember my covenant with thee in the days of thy youth, and I will establish with thee an everlasting Covenant. And thou shalt remember thy ways and be ashamed, when thou shalt receive thy sisters, thy elder and thy younger, and I will give them to thee for daughters, but not by thy Covenant." In this way Jerusalem, capital of God's new people, receives the promise that it will be given other nations for daughters, namely, the pagans who live far removed from God and who until now have had no share in the divine promises. "I will establish my Covenant with thee; and thou shalt know that I am the Lord, that thou mayest remember and be confounded, and mayest no more open thy mouth because of thy confusion, when I shall be pacified toward thee for all that thou hast done, saith the Lord God" (Ez. 16:59-63).

The story became actual truth on the eve of the passion, when the Man, possessed of God's own heart, told His disciples in the cenacle: "Drink ye all of this. For this is my blood in the new covenant, which shall be shed for many unto the remission of sins" (Mt. 26:27-28).

The Old Testament stresses two of Yahweh's attributes, mercy and fidelity, or, as the Vulgate calls them less accurately, "grace and truth." "All the ways of Yahweh are mercy and fidelity to them that seek after his covenant and law" (Ps. 24:10). In Psalm 135, the chorus keeps repeating, "Praise ye the Lord, for he is good. His mercy endureth for ever." We take it, then, that divine mercy and fidelity characterize the message of the Old Testament. And this makes us realize better the force of St. John's terse, solemn declaration in the opening chapter of his Gospel: "Of his fullness we have all received, one grace after another. True, the law was given through Moses, but mercy and fidelity came through Jesus Christ" (Jn. 1:16-17). Whatever the prophets had sung concerning God's "mercy and fidelity" became a reality in the New Testament. We have no longer parables but actual fact; God came down in person to us and became man. "The Word was made flesh [that is, a plain, weak man as we are] and dwelt among us [as did Yahweh of old, with His people in the desert or in the holy of holies, on

Mount Sion], and we saw his glory [His divine presence, as on Mount Tabor or after the resurrection], the glory belonging to the only begotten of the Father, full of grace and truth [mercy and fidelity]" (Jn. 1:14).

Man finds it hard to believe in love, especially in a love which forgives and perseveres in the face of betrayal and infidelity. That is why He, who is the incarnate "grace and truth" of the Father, "the radiance of God's glory and the very image of His being" (Heb. 1:3), will speak so insistently of God's love for us. Luke has preserved three parables emphasizing the reality we dare not easily accept, the fact that God loves us with unceasing fidelity. Those are the parables of the lost sheep, the lost silver piece and the prodigal son (Lk. 15:3-32).

"And he said: 'A certain man had two sons. And the younger of them said to his father: "Father, give me the portion of substance that falleth to me." ' " To the Jews, the promised land was their inheritance, which they had received from God Himself. "And he divided unto them his substance. And not many days after, the younger son, gathering all together, went abroad into a far land." This was not the promised land but the country of the heathens that lay outside God's covenant. "And there he wasted his substance, living riotously." Saying this, our Lord refers in delicate terms to the sin graphically described by the prophet Ezechiel, the sin of "prostitution," signifying apostasy and revolt against God.

"And after he had spent all, there came a mighty famine in that country; and he began to be in want. And he went and cleaved to one of the citizens of that country. And he sent him into his farm to feed swine." Thanks to the latter discreet detail, the Apostles (who were Jews) and the simple people of Galilee were sufficiently given to understand into what state of degradation the young man had sunk; to a Jew, swine were unclean animals which he could not tend without defiling himself.

And he would fain have filled his belly with the husks the swine did eat; and no man gave unto him.

And returning to himself, he said: "How many hired servants in my father's house abound with bread, and I here perish with hunger! I will arise and will go to my father and say to him: Father, I have sinned against heaven [that is, against God] and before thee; I am not worthy to be called thy son; make me one of thy hired servants." Rising up, he came to his father.

And when he was yet a great way off, his father saw him, and was moved with compassion, and running to him fell upon his neck, and kissed him. And the son said to him: "Father, I have sinned against heaven and before thee; I am not now worthy to be called thy son." And the father said to his servants: "Bring forth quickly the first robe and put it on him, and put a ring on his hand [sign of a full reinstatement into his former rank], and shoes on his feet; and bring hither the fatted calf, and kill it, and let us eat and make merry: because this my son was dead and is come to life again, was lost and is found." And they began to be merry. [Lk. 15:11-24]

This Gospel passage is a favorite one with poets and preachers, and justly so. But they usually fail to call attention to what follows in the sacred text, which brings out the difficulty man experiences in acknowledging and accepting God's love. Who among our good Catholics, or for that matter among priests and religious, rejoices when hearing that a public sinner has been reconciled with God on his deathbed? Who in his heart shares the joy which fills the heart of the heavenly Father? Last-minute conversions are commented upon in sarcastic, inconsiderate terms. Such talk seems to betray a hidden regret that, unlike the deceased man, one has not dared to have one's fling on earth for fear of missing a safe arrival in the next world.

The elder brother of the prodigal son showed spite because of the great feast with which the younger brother's homecoming was celebrated.

And he was angry and would not go in. His father, therefore, coming out began to entreat him. And he answering said to his father: "Behold, for so many years do I serve thee, and I have never transgressed thy commandment; and yet thou hast never given me a kid to make merry with my friends; but as soon as this thy son is come, who has devoured his substance with harlots, thou hast killed the fatted calf."

But he said to him: "Son, thou art always with me, and all I have is thine. But it was fit that we should make merry and be glad, for thy brother was dead, and is come to life again; he was lost, and is found." [Lk. 15:28-32]

We cannot claim to be Christians unless we believe in God's love. "We have seen and do testify that the Father hath sent his Son to be the Savior of the world. Whoever shall confess that Jesus is the Son of God, God abideth in him, and he in God. [For thus] we have known and have believed the charity which God hath to us. God is charity; and he who abideth in charity, abideth in God, and God in him." Then come the words which, according to St. Augustine, sum up the secret of grace: "Let us therefore love God, because God first hath loved us" (I Jn. 4:14-19).

The theology of grace is in the main the theology of God's love for us and of the love which God's first love has caused in us. *Grace* is the English word for the Latin *gratia*. Now, *gratia* has acquired many secondary meanings, both in the technical language of the theologians and in the usage of the Church and the great councils; but its prime Christian meaning comes from Scripture. The Latin Vulgate used *gratia* to translate the Greek word *charis*. All the sacred authors of the New Testament, Paul in particular, have borrowed from the Septuagint the term *charis* to render several Hebrew words conveying meanings reducible to three main ideas: condescending love, conciliatory compassion and fidelity. The basic sense of Christian grace, whatever its later and further technical or non-Scholastic connotations, should always remind us that God first loved us. Let that be its fundamental chord.

"Dearly beloved, let us love one another, for charity is of God. And every one that loveth is born of God and knoweth God. He that loveth not, knoweth not God; for God is charity. By this hath the charity of God appeared toward us, because God hath sent his only begotten Son into the world, that we may live by him. In this is charity: not as though we had loved God [by our power and means], but because he first loved us, and sent his Son to be a propitiation for our sins" (I Jn. 4:7-10).

The Covenant of Grace

The first part of this book has shown us that any deeper study of the faith must begin with an attitude of attention to what God tells us in the Church, in Holy Scripture and in Tradition. We take for granted that our first parable has caused in us the required attentive attitude and has prepared us to lend an ear to God's own stories concerning Himself.

Here we need do no more than recall to mind the leading ideas of Scripture, to which the preceding pages serve as introduction.

The Old Testament is but one long hymn of praise to the love which God showed to His chosen people, Israel. Whenever it describes the divine predilection, the central theme is always the covenant which God freely entered upon with His people. Around this central theme many others group themselves and swell into a powerful polyphony, as for instance God's fidelity and compassion, His patience and forbearance, His love and mercy. God is celebrated in turn as the bridegroom dealing with a fickle and faithless bride, as the shepherd, the vinedresser planting and tending his vineyard, the physician, and the father and king.

Special emphasis is placed on the fact that the divine favor is totally undeserved. What need had God of Israel? "Not because you surpass all nations in number, is the Lord joined unto you and hath chosen you, for you are the fewest of any people; but because the Lord hath loved you and hath kept His oath . . ." (Dt. 7:7). He has loved Israel "because I am God and not man, the holy one in your midst" (Os. 11:9). "It is not because of you . . . but for my holy name's sake" (Ez. 36:22). With good reason the psalmist exclaims, "Not to us, O Lord, not to us; but to thy name give glory. For thy mercy and for thy truth's sake, lest the Gentiles should say: Where is their God?" (Ps. 113:1-2).

God Himself—His sanctity—is the motive of His love. The Old Testament never stops underlining the absolute gratuitousness of the divine gift. While Israel keeps forfeiting the Lord's love by its repeated revolts, infidelities and idolatry, God remains true to His covenant; His word remains forever: He is God and not a man.

In pre-Christian times, the outstanding fact connected with man's salvation was precisely the covenant God had concluded with an insignificant nation, the prelude and preparation for the everlasting covenant made in His Son. All the other facts stand grouped around it. Before all else, creation clearly signifies that everything comes from God as a pure gift of love. After it rank all the memorable events which we learned in the Bible history of our schooldays, the exact bearing of which lay in great part beyond our youthful understanding. Among these events we may mark out the divine promises made to the patriarchs, the calling of Abraham, Israel's deliverance from the bondage of Egypt as an exceptional testimony of God's enduring love, the special providence watching over the Jewish people during the reign of the kings and the period of the prophets. Israel was not only too small and too insignificant a nation to warrant the slightest claim to a special selection, but its increasingly great infidelity and apostasy, its impenitence and obduracy caused it to forfeit all appearance of a claim to it. That is why the main mission of the prophets consisted in proclaiming God's absolute fidelity to His promises, the excellence of His love. They threatened that if Israel kept failing in its allegiance, God would reserve to Himself a "remnant," and transfer His choice to the poor and the contemptible; He would turn to other nations and make those "poor of Yahweh" henceforth the object of His election. It is not God who abandoned man, but man who abandoned God.

All that God wanted to be to Israel is but a distant foreshadowing of what He actually is to His "new people," to the "poor of Yahweh," to the Church. "For God so loved the world that he hath given his only begotten Son" (Jn. 3:16). Herein lies that other element of salvation with which the Christian epoch opened. The unique love of the Father was made manifest to us in Jesus Christ, not so much in spoken words as in deeds: the small, daily marvels narrated in the Gospels, but above all the final consummation of the cross.

The crowning act of the cross has become fully intelligible as a historical reality to our faith because of what immediately followed it. Two facts powerfully impressed the nascent Christian community: first, Christ's resurrection and ascension; second, the coming of the Holy Spirit, together with the wonders of spiritual fulfillment and enthusiasm which in the beginning of the primitive Church accompanied this descent and made it visible and tangible.

These realities have not failed to throw light even on the history of the Jewish people, God's chosen race. Whatever happened to Israel was intended by God as a portent, a preparation and a foreshadowing of the central fact of all history: that God Himself, in the person of His eternal Word, "was made flesh and dwelt among us" (Jn. 1:14), so that we in our turn might (in the bold language of the Greek Fathers) become gods, that is, filled with divine and filial life. St. John pointed this out when he disclosed the higher meaning of Caiphas' prophesy: "Do you not realize that it is good for you that one man should die for the people and not let the whole nation perish?" (Jn. 11:50). Caiphas had addressed those words to the Sanhedrin, but John was prompt to reveal the more hidden sense God meant them to convey: "Now, he did not say that of himself, but being the high priest of that year, he prophesied that Jesus should die for the nation; and not only for the nation, but to gather together in one the children of God that were dispersed" (Jn. 11:51-52).

The Apostle was more explicit still in his Epistle: "Behold what manner of charity the Father hath bestowed upon us that we should be called and should be sons of God. Therefore the world knoweth not us, because it knew him not. Dearly beloved, we are now the sons of God; and it hath not yet appeared what we shall be [that is, what it means to be sons of God has not yet been made known]. We know that when he shall appear, we shall be like to him: because we shall see him as he is" (I Jn. 3:1-2).

Sin and Love

These facts bring us still deeper into the redeeming truths of our faith—dogmas and articles of faith so frowned upon today in some circles. We are not here presented with abstract postulates, belonging to some sort of pious geometry, with axioms fettering creative thought in chains of arid speculation. It is true that faith restrains thought within certain limits, but like all original truth it both restrains and stimulates through the facts.

These facts, voices of God's perennial youth, deliver their enduring message not so much to discursive speculative reason as to the whole man. They lend fertility to thought by leading progressively to fresh, richer and deeper realizations. At the same time, they demand an unambiguous acceptance of their truth, the radiance of divine actuality. Take the Creed, for instance, the summary of Catholic belief: starting with creation, it proceeds like a triumphal march of divine deeds which, from creation till life everlasting, God has done for His people, His Church in general and each one of her members in particular. Thanks to these salvific facts, we are given to understand in what manner it is salvific or in what manner God grants us His grace.

The mystery of grace is the mystery of the way God's love

acts with us and for us. Considered as mere creatures, we stand in dire poverty outside the pale of the divine, almighty splendor. We may call that our creaturely isolation from God. Original sin, which our own personal sins actualize still further in life, relegates us not only out of God's glory but under God's wrath. Our creaturely condition is not merely destitute but stained and injured. As we are all born with original sin in our souls, we come on earth in the state of perdition.

Let us understand this well. Original sin in us is no personal, actual sin of ours, but is a state of estrangement from God and of perdition, affecting before God the whole of mankind. God sees us not as isolated individuals but as sharing a responsibility in common. We all fell away from the love of God into perdition with the whole of mankind.

Shakespeare exclaims in *Measure for Measure* (II, ii, 116-121):

> . . . but man, proud man,
> Dress'd in a little brief authority,
> Most ignorant of what he's most assured—
> His glassy essence—like an angry ape
> Plays such fantastic tricks before high heaven
> As make the angels weep. . . .

These lines are not merely poetic fantasy. The brutalizing experiences of our age have fortunately freed us from the smug, bourgeois conviction that human progress is inevitable. For all that, recent history can give us no more than vague evidence to connect these events with original sin. Taken in themselves, they could be explained on purely natural grounds; they could even be excused and dismissed as commonplace in the context of man's whole history.

If we are committed to the dogma of original sin, that is, to our common state of perdition in the sight of God, we will see that this belief rests mainly on a single fact, the cardinal event of our faith: Christ died for us all. The cross proves to us that we all need to be saved, and that the gift of reconciliation with God is offered and granted to all of us. The Church has merely attempted to define that basic historical fact in unambiguous words.

There is more still. The cross reveals to us that God had pity on us, that He came in search of us in our state of perdition and estrangement from Him, that in His fidelity and mercy He never lost sight of us, that He still loves us with a fatherly heart. *And that is grace.*

Grace is not something that hangs high above our heads like the aurora borealis on a frosty night. Grace comes down on us like an abundant dew, permeating us, or like the first breath of spring that stirs nature and awakens it. From grace, that is, from the power and warmth of God's initial love, we are made able to look up to Him once again. We know that through faith we are raised, attracted and driven toward Him in sorrow and reciprocation of love. Once again we have obtained the right to live as children of God. Together in and with Christ's filial love, there is born in us a new filial power enabling us, in union with Him and through the strength of the Spirit, to cry in very deed and truth, "Abba! Father!" (Rom. 8:15).

To grasp the significance of divine grace in all its fullness and depth, we might conceive of it as two parallel currents moving in opposite directions, one streaming down from God to us, the other returning with Christ to God. Blessed Jan van Ruysbroeck painted his mystical and theological system on the solid canvas of this truth. To him the work of grace is the mighty ebb and flow of the eternal trinitarian life. It comes down oceanlike from the Godhead, flooding the world to bring it fertility; it then returns to its source carrying all things in its sweep back to the infinite majestic glory of the Trinity.

Understand now: man shall go out and observe God in His glories with all His saints; and he shall contemplate the riches and the mercy with which God flows, with glories and with Himself and with incomprehensible delights, in all His saints, according to the desire of every spirit. [And man shall see] how the saints themselves, together with all they have received and with all they can do, flow back into that same rich, unique source from which all delight proceeds. This flowing of God demands always a flowing back again; for God is like a sea, ebbing and flowing, ceaselessly flowing into each one of His elect, according to the needs and the worth of each. And in His ebbing He draws back again all men to whom He has given in heaven and on earth, with all they have and all of which they are capable. And from such men He demands more than they can achieve. For He reveals Himself so rich and so merciful and so immeasurably good! And in this manifestation He demands of them love and honour according to His worth. God indeed desires to be loved by us in accordance with His excellence; in this, however, all spirits fail. And so, love is without manner and without fashion. For our spirits do not know how to add yet more to the love that they already bear; for each spirit's capacity for love is finite. And therefore the work of love is constantly begun afresh, so that God may be loved as He demands and as they desire.[1]

Grace, seen from God's side, signifies that God loves us gratuitously. His love is totally undeserved, first, because as creatures we can lay no claim to any right before God, and second, because our solidarity in evil has caused us to lose without appeal all the privileges God granted to mankind in the beginning. Again, His love is undeserved because in the last analysis all love must find in itself the justifying reason for its existence, and this is supremely the case with God's sovereign love. He loves because He is God and not man, because of His glory and the sanctity of His name.

God's assurance of His love is never an empty one. "As the rain and the snow come down from heaven and return no more thither but soak the earth and water it, and make it to be fertile and to give seed to the sower and bread to the eater: so shall my word coming forth from my mouth; it shall not return to me void, but it shall do whatever I please, and shall prosper in the things for which I sent it" (Is. 55:10-11). Consequently, grace, seen from man's side, is a created gift which brings him an inner strength, a lifting urge, a yearning for God. It lays hold of us in the innermost depth of our person, whence it fecundates the multiple regions of our life and blossoms visibly in deeds of holiness, of goodness and joy.

Now, divine grace, which flows out from God, is an interior compulsion or driving of the Holy Ghost Who, from within us, drives our spirit and incites it in all virtues. This grace flows from within us and not from outside. For God is more truly within us than we ourselves, and His inward driving and urging, natural or supernatural, is closer to us and more interior than our own deeds. And therefore, God works in us from inside outwards, while all creatures work from outside inwards. And because of this, grace and all

[1] Jan van Ruysbroeck, *Die Gheestelike Brulocht*, tr. Eric Colledge as *The Spiritual Espousals* (London: Faber & Faber, 1952), pp. 127–128.

divine gifts and God's inspirations come from within the unity of our spirit, and not from without through the senses and its images.[2]

St. Augustine expressed this double aspect of grace in the terse formula, *"Quia me amasti, fecisti me amabilem,"* "Because You have loved me, You have made me lovable"— and good. God's love has struck us; its wound burns in our hearts until it is healed in God. As St. Augustine said in his celebrated sentence, "You have made us [in creation and redemption] and turned us toward You, Lord, and our heart finds no peace until it rests in You."

Grace, a Presence of God

We are now in a position to enter a little more deeply into the mystery of grace. It is to our advantage that exact thought should be given an entry into the vast sphere of this mystery—though on the condition that we not attempt to debase its secrets by the crude light of our reasoning intelligence, or pretend to measure with the petty yardstick of our reason "what is the breadth and length and height and depth" of God's love (Eph. 3:18). It remains our duty, however, to try to learn our faith better. Respect of God and awe of the divine remoteness do not dispense us from attempting to grasp the momentous meaning of grace in human life. When we make this attempt, we are no longer dealing with Revelation properly speaking but with constructions of the human mind, which are wretched and rickety at best; whatever solidity they have is ultimately borrowed from the certainty of Revelation.

In unraveling the mystery of grace, we find a most appropriate scheme of thought in personalistic philosophy, especially in the description of the presence of one person to another. Grace in general can be described as the secret of God's presence in our life. And in explaining it this way, we are convinced that we are faithfully following the Master's own teaching. Christ considered no legacy more precious to His Church than His abiding presence with us

2 *Ibid.,* p. 21.

through the Spirit: "Again I say to you, that if two of you shall consent upon earth concerning anything, whatsoever they shall ask, it shall be done to them by my Father who is in heaven. For where there are two or three gathered together in my name, there am I in the midst of them" (Mt. 18:19-20). St. Matthew's Gospel closes with the assurance of an everlasting presence: "Behold, I am with you . . . even to the consummation of the world" (Mt. 28:20). We also have the words Christ spoke in the farewell discourse after the last supper: "If any one loves me, he will keep my word, and my Father will love him, and we will come to him and will make our abode with him" (Jn. 14:23). These words are followed immediately by the parable of the vine and the branches (Jn. 15:1-8).

The early Christians did not forget Christ's solemn promise, even in times of persecution. As baptized and believing disciples of our Lord, they knew they were no longer living alone, not even when undergoing abuse and scorn. "You shall greatly rejoice," Peter told them, "if you now must be for a little time made sorrowful in diverse temptations: that the test of your faith (much more precious than gold which is tried by fire) may be found unto praise and glory and honor at the coming of Jesus Christ" (I Pt. 1:6-7). The chapter continues, "Whom having not seen, you love: in whom also now, though you see him not, you believe and, believing, shall rejoice with joy unspeakable and glorified; receiving the end of your faith, even the salvation of your souls" (I Pt. 1:8-9).

Faith, then, aims always at securing Christ's presence in our life—an inner, actual presence overflowing with joy through the veil of faith. This is the sense in which we accept Christ's words addressed to Thomas: "Because you have seen me, Thomas, you have believed [in Christ's resurrection and consequent omnipresence]. Blessed are they [both at the time the Gospels were written and ever since] that have not seen and have believed" (Jn. 20:29).

Grace is the mystery of God's intense, living presence in us. The allegory with which we opened this chapter described this personal reality in terms of psychology and human love. But when we come to consider God and man, we are immediately confronted with a very different matter, simply because God's relations with men do not correspond to men's relations with God or to the relations of men among themselves. The relations between God and men are not the same from both sides and are therefore not interchangeable, though this is the case among men. For instance, we might just as well have told the story of a straying young man who is saved through a girl's pure love.

We should guard against the assumption that man can give or offer anything to God—whether love or joy, pain, homage or holiness—that he has not first received as a gift from God. What is more, when man does freely return the divine gifts to the Father, he does so not by himself alone but together with God, that is, with Christ and the Holy Ghost. These precisions have their importance, for the reason that a Protestant might say that in the domain of grace Catholics assume a presumptive and arrogant attitude before God, considering themselves almost His equals. We Catholics, some might allege, seem to think the divine majesty is indebted to us through our good works and merits. There may indeed be Catholics who in their conduct or teaching lay themselves open to such a charge. But when this happens, we do not hesitate to affirm that their behavior amounts to a perversion of the faith, to a camouflaged sin of Pharisaic pride. To the Corinthians, Paul said very tellingly, "What have you that you have not received?" (I Cor. 4:7).

With these precautions in mind, we may now proceed with the theological consideration of grace as the mystery of the *living* presence of one person to another.

On one side stands the Godhead in three Persons, Father, Son and Holy Ghost; on the other side we stand, creatures and sinners, but despite this made into the image of God. Veiled in His providence, God speaks to us in every one of the daily events and in the concrete situation of the life He has chosen for us. He speaks to us through the Church and also, without intermediary, in our hearts. He speaks to man with love. He calls each one by his own name, and this name expresses both a commission and a vocation. His word confers upon man the condition, new and peculiarly his own, of being a "you" before God; and here as always, God's word is operative and creative. The Father speaks to me as to a "you," as to his trusted child reborn and risen already. God's word affects me in the deepest depth of my self; He confers upon this personal core in me a density and firmness never suspected before. I am truly *some one* before God

because He speaks to me. This is the essential of that creative presence of God in the soul through grace.

Our Union With Christ

Grace, a Likeness to Christ

Properly speaking, it is not we who by grace stand before
God. God's life of love is of itself a unique and intense
presence of God to Himself. The Father stands in perfect
self-identity, power and density before the Son; so does the
Son stand before the Father; and so do the Father and the
Son before the Holy Ghost. With this in our minds, we
may describe the mystery of grace more accurately by saying that through grace man, while still on earth, is introduced, in a hidden though real manner, into the glorious
intimacy belonging to the Father, the Son and the Holy
Ghost. Our presence of God is a *co*-presence. It is as if
through grace, through the loving election of the Father, we
are lifted up to the level of the Son. Grace signifies that by
God's sheer love and mercy we are permitted to stand before
the Father with and in the Son and in the power of the
Holy Ghost. It means that we share in the loving converse
of the divine Persons. The core of our personality is
spiritually raised to a re-created density and self-identity
(whence the term *supernatural*) enveloped in the unique
density and self-identity of the Son.

Insofar as the life of grace on earth is already a beginning and an actual foretaste of paradise, what will constitute life eternal is already present in germ—the possibility
of living and abiding in the all-surpassing intimacy of the
divine Persons. To return to the comparison made earlier,
through grace, each one of us is like a drop of water lost
in the mighty ebb and flow of the divine ocean; diffused in
the divine life, we are enabled for the first time to be ourselves in a unique way—ourselves, just because we have
become greater than ourselves.

The Son, Image of the Father

Holy Scripture presents the Son to us as the visible Revelation of the Father, as Him in Whom the Father created the world. "In the beginning was the Word, and the Word was with God, and the Word was God. He was in the beginning with God. All things came into being through him and nothing whatever came into being without him. . . . No one has ever seen God [the Father]; the only begotten God [the Son] who is in the bosom of the Father has made him known" (Jn. 1:1-3, 18).

Soaring to equal heights, the unknown author of the Epistle to the Hebrews introduced the Son in similar terms: "After God had spoken of old to our fathers through the prophets, he has at last spoken to us these days through his Son, [through] him whom he destined to be heir of all things, and through whom he made the universe. He, the effulgence of God's glory and the perfect image of his substance, upholds the universe by the power of the divine mandate . . ." (Heb. 1:1-3).

A few years earlier, Paul the Apostle had written to the Colossians:

He is the image of the invisible God, the firstborn of all creatures. For in him all things were created, whether in the heavens or on the earth, what is visible or invisible, whether Thrones or Dominations, Principalities or Powers. All things have been created through him and for him. He exists before all things, and in him all things subsist. He is also the head of the body, which is the Church. He is the beginning, the firstborn among the dead, so that in all things He may hold the preeminence; for it has pleased [the Father] that in him should dwell the fullness [of the Father] and that, through him, he should reconcile all things to himself, whether the things that are on earth, or things in the heavens, making peace by the blood of his cross. [Col. 1:15-20]

In creation and in redemption, the Son stands first. He is the image of the Father, and in the likeness of this image the Father has created and redeemed all things. This is the pivotal fact in the whole history of our salvation.

The Countenance of the Son

The ancient Fathers of the Church keenly perceived the unique place held by the Son in both creation and redemption; and they kept it constantly in mind when they drew up the fundamental tenets of their theology. To them nothing was clearer than that man has been created in the image of the Son, and in that same image has been re-created in grace.

For a closer acquaintance with this divine prototype, we shall listen once more to Holy Scripture. Christ spoke of Himself as the Son of Man, the true Servant of Yahweh, and the only begotten Son of the Father.

The name *Son of Man* means nothing more than *man* in the original Hebrew. But this primary meaning, never to be lost sight of, was given an additional connotation by Christ Himself after the glorification on Mount Tabor when He connected it with the two ideas of the suffering servant of Yahweh and the mysterious "son of man" who, according to Daniel's prophesy, "appears on the clouds of heaven" (Dn. 7:13).

Perhaps the finest pages in the Old Testament were written by the unknown author, generally called Deutero Isaias, of the Book of Consolation (Is. 40-55). The central figure of that book is the servant of Yahweh who is to deliver Israel from sin through his sufferings. That is why the unknown author earned for himself the title of "the fifth evangelist."

Christ Himself acknowledged at some decisive moments of His life that He was the Servant of Yahweh foretold in Isaias. One Sabbath day in the synagogue at Nazareth, He was invited to stand up and read a passage from Scripture. A scroll of the prophet Isaias was handed to Him. He unrolled it and found the place where it read: "The Spirit of the Lord is upon me, because he has anointed me. He has sent me out to bring the glad tidings to the poor, to announce freedom to the prisoners and sight to the blind, to set the oppressed at liberty, to proclaim a year of grace when men may find acceptance with the Lord" (Is. 61:1-2; written either by Deutero-Isaias or by one of his disciples). Then He rolled up the scroll, returned it to the attendant and sat down. The eyes of all in the synagogue were fixed upon Him. He then said to them: "This passage of Scripture, which you have just heard, has been fulfilled today" (Lk. 4:21).

We find in the New Testament not only a number of passages taken from the Book of Consolation but also many characteristic allusions to a Christology, still in the making at the time the New Testament was being written, and largely based on quotations from Deutero-Isaias. For instance, "Behold, the lamb of God, who takes away the sin of the world!" (Jn. 1:29), and "In Him, God has been well pleased."

We know that St. John built his own theology on Christ's death and resurrection. " 'If only I am lifted up from the earth, I will attract all men to myself.' In saying this, he signified the nature of the death he was about to die" (Jn. 12:32; see also 3:14; 8:28). It is perhaps less generally known that "being lifted up"—a symbol of the cross, the resurrection and ascension, that is, of all the essential events entering into the work of the redemption—is also a reference to the best-known prophecy of Deutero-Isaias regarding the suffering and triumph of the Servant of Yahweh: "Behold, my servant shall prosper; he shall be lifted up and shall be as greatly exalted as many were appalled at him. For his appearance was debased beneath that of man, and his form beneath that of the sons of men. But many nations shall be amazed at him, and kings shall shut their mouths before him. . . . He shall have a posterity, he shall prolong his days; and what is pleasing to Yahweh will be accomplished in him" (Is. 52:13-15; 53:10).

Some years before St. John wrote, Paul described the theology of redemption in his Epistle to the Philippians, though in his own personal manner and according to his own cast of mind:

Keep those sentiments among you which you see in Christ Jesus; he, though subsisting in the form of God, did not cling to the likeness with God as to a prey [as did Adam and Eve]. But he emptied himself, taking to himself the form of servant (Is. 53:3, 11-12) and thus becoming like to man [Son of Man]. Appearing as man, he had humbled himself by being obedient unto death, even to the death of the cross. And, therefore, God has lifted him up and has bestowed upon him the name above all names. . . . Jesus Christ is the Lord. [Phil. 2:5-11]

The servant is one who obeys, who does the will of the Father, whose bread it is to accomplish the will of the Father. Christ would later pray, "not my will, but yours be done" (Mt. 26:39). Thus, the trait most characteristic of a servant is obedience. And it is through obedience that Christ saved us (Rom. 5:19). We men had sinned, and through sin had become disobedient. Christ wanted to be in the world what we, according to the mind of the Father, should have been from the beginning, God's obedient servants.

The third characteristic expression Christ used for Himself was "Son of the Father." *Son,* in both Hebrew and Aramaic, can stand for more than one form of relationship —to a person or a people, to God or the devil. Toward the end of His life, Christ gave this rather vague word a clear-cut meaning by applying it to Himself in order to mark the intimate connection He has with the Father. Later, both Paul and John determined this sense still further, and spoke of Christ as God's "own Son" and God's "only begotten Son." Now, what is most characteristic of a son is *love.* God is love, and in Christ that love came down to this earth (I Jn. 4:7; 5:4); through His love He saved the world. Sin is essentially self-seeking, a hardening of the heart and pride. Love alone can destroy the power of sin. Christ proved to us the earnestness and intensity of His love by dying on the cross (Jn. 15:13; Rom. 5:5-8; Gal. 2:20).

In the Image of the Son

Here we have to take into account a form of thought quite special to the Hebrew mind. Hebrew thinking did not proceed along abstract, metaphysical lines as does Western, which is molded upon the pattern left us by the Greeks. It dealt always in concrete terms, and showed a marked preference for symbols and images. Exegetes have discovered that in the Old Testament, and consequently also in the New, the idea of "sharing" is often expressed by what has come to be called the "corporate personality." What is said of one person can often be applied to the nation to which that person belongs. This literary genre is often used in the Book of Consolation. In some verses, the Servant of Yahweh is no longer simply the mysterious person described by Isaias, but is also Israel itself as a people; if it is to share in his consolation and triumph, it must share in his sufferings.

That is certainly the way Paul and John understood matters from the start. To them it was perfectly certain that if Christ was the Servant, we had all become servants and slaves of God in Him. And this was so real that in Paul's mind it constituted the special title of honor for all Christians. St. John pointed to the fact that we have become children of God in and through the Son: "To those who received him and to those who believed in his name, he gave the power of becoming children of God. They are not born of blood, nor from carnal desire, nor from the will of man, but they are born from God" (Jn. 1:12-13). On another page of his Gospel, the same evangelist reported Caiphas' prophecy concerning Christ's passion, and he was at pains to explain at once the import of those prophetic words. It was an occasion for him to indicate the meaning of both redemption and grace. "He did not say that of himself; but being the high priest of that year, he prophesied that Jesus was to die for the nation; and not for the nation only, but also that he might gather together the scattered children of God" (Jn. 11:51-52).

In his first Epistle, John wrote, "Whoever is born of God does not sin, because the seed [of God] remains in him; and he cannot sin, since he is born of God. By this are the children of God and the children of the devil known apart: whoever does not live right is not of God, at least not he who does not love his brethren" (I Jn. 3:8-10). In the beginning of that same chapter the Apostle said, "See how God has shown his love toward us: that we should be called children of God, and should be his children! Beloved, we are already children of God, but as yet it has not been made known what we shall be hereafter. We know, however, that when he will appear [on the last day] we shall be like him, because we shall see him as he is" (I Jn. 3:1-2).

These words are a striking affirmation of our divine sonship. But St. John was not alone in his affirmation—Paul was equally emphatic: "All those who let themselves be led by the Spirit of God, they are the sons of God. The Spirit which you have received is not one of slavery, leading again to fear. But you have received the Spirit of adoption which makes us cry, 'Abba! Father!' The Spirit bears witness to our spirit that we are children of God; and if children, then also heirs of God and heirs with Christ, since we share in his sufferings in order to share in his glorification" (Rom. 8:14-17). In his Epistle to the Galatians, Paul connected our participation in the divine sonship yet more explicitly with the redemption and therefore with grace:

We, too, when we were still minors, were serving in subjection to the elements of this world. But when the appointed time had come, God [the Father] sent out his Son on a mission to us, to be born from a woman and subjected to the Law [of the Jews], in order that he might set free those who were subject to the Law and that we might become sons of adoption. And because you are sons, God has sent into our hearts the Spirit of his Son, crying, "Abba, Father." You are, therefore, no longer a slave [of the Law]; you are a son; and if a son, then also an heir by God's act. [Gal. 4:3-7]

"Abba, Father": these two words are not unlike the opening words of the Aramaic Our Father, the prayer taught us by Christ in person. In this case, we cannot in truth recite the Our Father unless our spirit has a share in the Spirit of God. In the Hebrew idiom, and thus also in biblical Greek, the term *spirit* does not designate the spiritual principle of the human compound. In the first place, it signifies the Spirit and the power of God Himself, the One who later on would reveal Himself as the Person of the Holy Ghost. In the second place, it means the gifts made by the Spirit, but more especially the whole man, that is, body and soul living as one person, insofar as these are filled with the Holy Ghost and consequently totally transformed. In this sense, *spirit* stands in opposition to *flesh;* and *flesh,* in Paul's writings, means the whole man insofar as he is creature, insofar especially as he is a sinner separated from God.

If we can grasp this usage in the sense intended by Paul, John and the other evangelists, we are in possession of the beginnings of a theology of grace. Briefly put, it would amount to this: away from God and as a creature estranged from God, especially if lost through sin, man is nothing more than "flesh." But through the power of God's Spirit—the

Spirit of Christ—sinful man becomes "spirit," totally and utterly renewed by God's Spirit. Then and only then does what he has indeed become appear: child of God and heir of God, with and in and through Christ Jesus.

The Apostle Peter summarized this in the well-known text, "Whatever is necessary to life and piety, the divine power has bestowed upon us, together with the knowledge of him who called us by his glory and virtue. He has granted us thereby his high and precious promises, so that, leaving behind the corruption of this world with its evil passions, you may share in the divine nature . . ." (II Pt. 1:3-4). Exegetes are probably right in saying that Peter was not thinking at all of the somewhat forced theological meaning which we tend to read in his words today. Nonetheless, Peter's is a bold affirmation. Paul and the author of the Epistle to the Hebrews touched upon the same idea:

The Lord is the spirit, and where the Spirit of the Lord is, there is freedom. To all of us it has been given to see with unveiled face the glory of the Lord, and to be transfigured into an ever-increasing glorious image of him; for it is the Spirit of the Lord who works this out. [II Cor. 3:17-18]

Put on the new man, the one created in the image of God, in justice and holiness. [Eph. 4:24]

They [our fathers according to the flesh] have corrected us for a short while [in our youth], at their own caprice; but he does so for our advantage, in order that we may share in his sanctity. [Heb. 12:10]

These numerous affirmations in the New Testament are a continuation of a much older tradition which identifies likeness to God with imitation of God in our daily life. Here is what Christ said in the Sermon on the Mount: "But I tell you: love your enemies, pray for those who persecute you; so that you may be children of your Father who is in heaven, who causes his sun to rise upon good and evil, and causes rain to fall upon the just and the unjust. For, if you love only those who love you, what claim have you to a reward? . . . Be perfect as your heavenly Father is perfect" (Mt. 5:44-48). To Israel of old, Yahweh, in the book of Leviticus, had set the same high standard of conduct: "Be holy because I, Yahweh your God, am holy" (Lv. 19:2).

Christ, Prototype of Our Grace

A good many of our modern theological textbooks enlarge upon the idea of our "assimilation in God" along rather abstract lines, very much as if it were a likeness to the Godhead, to the divine nature as such. But in the light of biblical teaching this notion makes little sense, especially since the word *God* in the New Testament is usually intended to designate God the Father. The theology of God, as found in the Old Testament, has been shifted into that of the Father in the New. As later councils would summarize matters, the Father is the primordial source of all that is divine. But this rather attenuated tradition has the disadvantage of neglecting what is properly original and unique in the history of our salvation—that we have been re-created in and through the Son, the image of the Father. Likeness to God is thus fundamentally coincident with likeness to the Son. And this precisely is the essential characteristic which both the divine indwelling and grace develop in us.

The early Fathers, who as bishops guided and taught the Church, never neglected this truth. It constitutes also one of the most rewarding insights of our mystical tradition. These themes did not escape Ruysbroeck, a man steeped in and nourished on the reading of Scripture. We have been created, and through grace we have been reborn in the image of the Son. In the eyes of our mystic, this is not just an abstract thought; it is something concrete, actual, something intimately bound up with the history of the redemption. In his book *The Perfection of the Sons of God*, he made use of the figurative language of the Bible to designate the various steps of the ladder to Christian perfection. In this respect, he remained of course a man of the Middle Ages, but not for a moment did he forget that Holy Writ uses those various figures of speech to define what forms the essence of all Christian life.

If we could renounce ourselves and all that is ours in our works, from the moment we come into our naked and imageless spirit [that is, into the depth of our person, where, stripped and freed from images, we are in immediate contact with the Spirit of God] we would reach beyond all things. And in this nakedness, we would be guided, without any intermediary, by the Spirit of God, and would feel the assurance that we are truly sons of God [the highest step we can reach in the Christian life]; for, as says St. Paul, God's own Apostle, "Those who are guided by the Spirit of God are the sons of God." You should know, nevertheless, that all good believing men are sons of God. For they were all born of the Spirit of God, and the Spirit of God lives in them all; and He moves and urges each individual according to his habitual disposition to virtue and good works wherein God is well pleased. But because men do not turn themselves to God in an equal degree, I shall call some of them faithful servants, others intimate friends, and still others hidden sons. And yet all are servants, friends and sons; for they all serve and love and attend to the one God; and all live and operate by the Spirit of God.[3]

A little while ago, we spoke of the notion of the "corporate personality" as typical of the scriptural way of thinking. It is interesting to note how Ruysbroeck very naturally applies to all Christians the words God the Father spoke on Mount Tabor (which are taken, incidentally, from Isaias): "All those who follow our Lord Jesus Christ hear the voice of the Father, for of them all He says, 'These are My chosen sons, in whom I am well pleased.' Each one of these beloved ones receives grace according to the measure and in the manner that please Him."[4]

In another page of Ruysbroeck, from *A Mirror of Eternal Blessedness*, we find a passage still more closely related to the teaching of Scripture:

We have also to overcome our senses, to conquer our nature, to carry our cross and to follow after Christ. In this way we repay to Him the debt which He paid for us. Through His death and voluntary penance, we have been made one with Him and [have become] His faithful servants, and we belong to His Kingdom. When we die to our will by accomplishing His will, and when His will becomes our will, then we are His disciples and His chosen friends. More still, when we are raised up through love and when our

[3] Jan van Ruysbroeck, *Vanden Blinckenden Steen* (*The Perfection of the Sons of God*), in *Werken* (4 vols.; Tielt: Lannoo, 1946-1948), III, p. 21.

[4] *Ibid.*, p. 38.

minds stand naked and imageless, just as God made them, then we are formed by the Holy Ghost and are sons of God. Mark these words and sentences and live up to them.

When Christ, the Son of God, willed to die for love of us, He surrendered His life into the hands of His enemies till death. And that is how he was the obedient Servant of His Father and of all the world. He surrendered also His own will to the will of the Father, and by doing so He practiced the highest justice and taught all truth. He raised His Spirit in most blissful delight and said, "It is all fulfilled"; "Father, into your hands I commend my spirit." Continuing the same verse, the prophet David, in the name of all good men who follow Christ, seems to reply, "Lord, God of truth, you have set me free" (Ps. 30:6). For indeed we cannot set ourselves free. But when we follow Christ, as I have shown above, with all the means at our disposal, our works become one with His works and are ennobled through grace. That is how He has redeemed us, not indeed through our works but in His works; in His merits He has set us free and has redeemed us.

But if we would feel and possess that freedom, His Spirit must consume our spirit in love and sink it into the bottom-less well of His grace and liberal goodness. There our spirit is baptized, set free and made one with His Spirit. . . . For the will of God has become our will; and that is the root of all true love. When we are born anew of God's Spirit, then our will is free, for it is made to be one with the free will of God. There our spirit, through love, is raised and taken up into one Spirit, one will, one freedom with God.[5]

Ruysbroeck calls this very sharing in Christ's fullness the "fullness of grace." "He has been given to us out of pure love; in His nature, He is the Son of love. If we are united to Him, we are sons, and in His Spirit we cry 'Abba, Father.' "[6] In a powerful passage, our mystic describes the full flowering of grace, and as a matter of course connects it with the history of salvation: "God's Truth [that is, Christ] speaks within our spirit: 'Look at Me as I look at you, rejoice in possessing Me as I rejoice in possessing you; and as I am you wholly and undivided, so I wish you to

[5] Jan van Ruysbroeck, *Spieghel der Eeuwigher Salicheit* (*A Mirror of Eternal Blessedness*), in *Werken*, III, pp. 144-146.

[6] Jan van Ruysbroeck, *Vanden Gheestelikken Tabernakel* (*The Spiritual Tabernacle*), in *Werken*, II, p. 110.

be Me wholly and undivided.' " [7] These words describe the relations with and in Christ which grace confers upon us during this life.

These relations are not to be thought of as independent from our personal history or the history of mankind. They all originate in the Son, the ultimate and exemplary cause of all creatures and grace: " 'I have seen you from all eternity and before all creation, in Me and one with Me and as Myself,' " which means that we were present from the start in the divine, exemplary cause of creation. " 'It is there that I have known you, loved you, called and chosen you.' " With this, our history starts on its course. From heaven, the image of the Son is imprinted on man: " 'I have created you in My likeness and image.' " And now the incarnation: " 'I have taken to Myself your nature and have imprinted on it My image, so that you might be one with Me, without intermediary, in the glory of My Father. I have created My soul with all its powers, and filled it with every gift, so that I could serve and obey your Father and My Father in the human nature we have in common, with all I had, till death. And out of My fullness of grace and gifts I have filled your soul and all its powers, in order that you may be like Me, and in My strength and in My gifts serve, thank and praise our God for endless eternity.' " [8]

This lifestream flows through us all as we are gathered into one body; it unites us all in Christ: "See now: we are all one with God in our eternal image, because the Wisdom of God [that is, the second Person of the Blessed Trinity] is He Who has taken to Himself the nature of us all. But though we are all one in our likeness to God because of the nature which He assumed, we have still to be like Him in grace and virtue if we want to find ourselves one with God in our eternal image, which is God Himself." That oneness and likeness with God the Father in and through the Son, our ultimate exemplar of all grace, is based on the mystery of the incarnation: "After this manner, the humanity of our Lord Jesus Christ was and is raised and made one with the Wisdom of God (the second Person); His soul and all its powers were filled and remain filled

---

[7] Jan van Ruysbroeck, *Vanden XII Beghinen* (*The Twelve Beguines*), in *Werken*, IV, pp. 15-16.

[8] *Ibid.*

with all graces. He is to us like a living fountain from which we draw whatever we need." [9]

At this point, Ruysbroeck speaks once more of the salvific significance of Christ's earthly life, death and resurrection. Then he passes on to the distribution of grace, dispensed in the Church and through the sacraments: " 'Mark well, beloved, what more I have done for you. I have given and bequeathed to you My flesh and living blood, to be food and drink of an all-pervading heavenly savor, and of a nature to suit the desire and taste and experience of every man. I have nourished your passions, your greed and life of the senses with My martyred, glorious body. I have nourished and filled your love and rational life with My Spirit, with My gifts and with the merits whereby I please My Father." This passage describes the renewal of our psychosomatic life, of our will and intellect. Ruysbroeck continues now with what is deepest and highest in man, namely, what we have called a person's core of density: " 'I have nourished and filled your prayer and contemplation with My personality, so that you might live in Me and I in you, God and man, in likeness of virtues and unity of blessedness. My Father and I have filled the world with Our Spirit, with Our gifts and with Our sacraments, according to the desire and needs of everyone. O man, consider Who I am and how I have lived for you and served you, and that I have suffered for you. Be grateful and answer Me according to all your capabilities.' " [10]

Six centuries later, in the Netherlands by the sea, of which Ruysbroeck spoke so willingly, Father Emile Mersch, the well-known theologian of the Mystical Body, renewed the theology of grace and summed it up in the striking title of his article *"Filii in Filio"*: grace makes us, each one individually and all in common, "sons of God in the Son." [11]

[9] *Ibid.*

[10] *Ibid.*, pp. 15-16.

[11] Émile Mersch, S. J., *"Filii in Filio,"* Nouvelle Revue Théologique, 1938, pp. 551-582, 681-702, 809-830. These articles were revised and reprinted in Emile Mersch, S. J., *"Filii in Filio:* The Life Imparted by the Trinity," The Theology of the *Mystical Body,* tr. Cyril Vollert, S. J. (St. Louis: B. Herder), pp. 325-374.

Conclusion

We would like to formulate a doctrine of grace in keeping with such a rich tradition; the best we can do for the moment is summarize the discussion above. Grace has its source in God. From all eternity, it has lain hidden in the very life of the Trinity. It comes to us insofar as God speaks to us in love, addresses to us His creating and recreating word of love, unites us to Himself in love, and thus establishes His presence in us.

By this divine presence the image of God is already prepared through creation; damaged by sin, it is healed and restored by the redemption and raised to greater heights and intensity than ever before.

There is no question here of an impersonal abstraction, an assimilation of man in the divine nature by means of a divine action in which the three Persons have no personal, characteristic part. Nor does the assimilation come about independently of our history of salvation; for in that history precisely, one of the divine Persons has and maintains His own particular role.

We have been redeemed in Christ. If so, it follows that the image of the Son, as He revealed Himself to be during His earthly life, is imprinted on us. For our sake, He became the obedient Servant of Yahweh. We in turn become by grace the faithful servants of Yahweh "through Him and with Him and in Him," as is said at the end of the canon of the mass. He lives here on earth as the loving Son of the Father; and we become adopted children of the Father.

The image which the gracious and grace-conferring divine presence imprints on us is thus a concrete one—concrete in its origin, in its formation, in the aim intended. In other words, we are the obedient servants in the Servant, loving children of God in the Son. It follows quite logically that, as soon as grace calls us, urging us to act in conformity with it, it spurs us on to live in "obedience to the faith" and to yield to the attraction of love. This twofold prompting expresses itself spontaneously in the practice of hope, a hope which we embody in our temporal life through all earthly hardships, dangers and struggles, and which helps us keep our gaze on the final fulfillment awaiting us after death.

In essence, the three theological virtues are simply the normal expression in our lives of what in fact we are in our innermost selves by grace: obedient servants and loving children. The theological virtues are the existential acceptance, the rooting and actualizing of what we are from the moment the Blessed Trinity comes to dwell in us, to unite us to Itself in a vital and creative presence and thus to let us share in Its life. By grace, heaven has begun. "At present, we are looking at a confused reflection in a mirror; but then, we shall see face to face" (I Cor. 13:12).

Our Union with the Father and the Holy Ghost

In explaining the concrete effects which the indwelling of the Blessed Trinity produces, we started from our union with Christ. Our union with the Father and the Holy Ghost does not fall into second place on that account, as if it were a mere consequence or secondary aspect of the first union; quite the contrary. It must ever remain the central fact of our faith that the Trinity has come down to us in the visibility of the Son. He is the Word of the Father, the paternal splendor, the Father's perfect image. The Son keeps the role He received in the order of grace as mediator in the redemption. The Son fills not two roles, therefore, but two aspects of one and the same phenomenon: God's dealings with man.

Of him it has been witnessed: You are a priest forever according to the order of Melchisedech. And so, a fuller hope has been brought into our lives, enabling us to draw closer to God. . . . In consequence, he can, for all time, give eternal salvation to those who approach God through him, since he is always living to intercede for them. [Heb. 7:17-25]

This is why he is the mediator of the new covenant; his

death has brought acquittal of all the transgressions under the old Law, so that those who are called may receive the promised eternal inheritance. [Heb. 9:15]

For God [always meaning God the Father in the New Testament] is one, and one also is the mediator between God and man, the man Jesus Christ, who gave himself as a ransom for them all. At the appointed time, he bore his witness; and of that wisdom I am the chosen herald, sent as an apostle—I make no false claims, I am only recalling the truth—to be a true and faithful teacher of the Gentiles. [I Tim. 2:5-7]

Union Without Intermediary

In and with the Son we return to the Father. Such is the teaching of Scripture. We shall satisfy ourselves with quoting the concluding portion of Paul's important chapter describing Christ's and our resurrection:

Christ has risen from the dead, the first-fruits of all those who have fallen asleep. For, since by a man death was brought to us, so by a man has come the resurrection of the dead. As all have died in Adam, so also in Christ all shall be made to live. But each one must rise in his own rank: Christ is the first-fruits, and then those that belong to Christ at his coming; after this the completion when he shall hand over the Kingdom to God the Father after he has abolished every other sort of rule, authority and power. . . . And when all things have been completely subjected, then the Son himself will be subject to the One who subjected all things to him, so that God may be all in all. [I Cor. 15:20-28]

The same truth is brought home to us by the liturgy. With few exceptions, all liturgical prayers are addressed to the Father through and with the Son in unity with the Holy Ghost. Prayer, and above all liturgical prayer, which reflects the faith of the Church in a far purer form than do most private prayers, is the living, personal expression of the order of grace in which we stand, by which we must live and to which we have to conform ourselves while praying.

It would be theologically incorrect to think that the immediate union of the Son with our souls, as described above, unites us with the Father and the Holy Ghost only mediately or derivatively. Because of the total mutual immanence of the divine Persons within the unity of the divine nature, we come through the Son into immediate contact with the Father and the Holy Ghost. The Father and the Holy Ghost live in us as really and immediately as the Son, notwithstanding the fact that fundamentally grace is granted to us in our quality of servants in the Servant and adopted children in the Son. It would be a serious mistake to look upon a divine Person as a means of reaching another divine Person by something like a second movement.

Medieval authors are known for their love of apt symbols. Touching on the mystery of the incarnation, they resorted to an illustration that throws some light on how that mystery is worked out and how the Person of the Word is united to His sacred humanity. We shall borrow their illustration and use it to explain to some extent the mystery of grace, so closely allied to the mystery of the incarnation.

Imagine, they said, three girls adorning one of themselves for marriage. All three are immediately engaged in the work of adorning, but only one, the bride, is being prepared for the wedding. To apply this to the incarnation, only the second Person of the Blessed Trinity, the Word, is "robed" in a humanity; but each one of the three Persons has His own immediate active part in working out the incarnation.

The same illustration throws some light on the pattern God follows in communicating His grace; for grace comes to us, along with salvation and redemption, in and through Christ. Fundamentally, the mystery of the incarnation and the mystery of divine grace conferred on man are two different things altogether; but in the language of theology, they have a real analogy. They possess a similarity in structure, because God has connected them closely with each other.

Christ called Himself, and let others call Him, Son of God. Man, too, in a state of grace, is to be called a son of God, but not on the same ground. Christ is the Son of God by nature, and therefore by right, while we are adopted sons, sharing in Christ's sonship. The divine activity which causes us to share in Christ's sonship must be thought of as a continuation of the very same divine activity which sent the Son on His earthly mission. From the days of St. Irenaeus, the Greek Fathers expressed this idea in the now-classical dictum that God became man in order that man might become "god." They called the mystery of grace the mystery of our *divinization*. Even today, the Eastern Orthodox use this terminology. We should like to see this grand and rich tradition spread again among the faithful.

Scripture teaches no other doctrine; it speaks frequently and equally of the indwelling of the three Persons and of the indwelling of the Father and of the Holy Ghost. The indwelling of the Holy Ghost is mentioned so often that the theology of the Schoolmen dealt with the dogma of grace as the mystery of the indwelling of the Holy Ghost. Scripture, of course, does not enter into technical precisions; but the writers were aware that the three Persons, each in His own characteristic manner, work out Their indwelling in us. We shall endeavor to examine in some detail what is proper to the action of the Father and to the action of the Holy Ghost.

St. John's Teaching

To begin with, we quote two passages from Holy Writ in which John and Paul passed, in the most natural way, from the indwelling of one Person to the presence of the others. In the farewell discourse after the last supper, as reported by John (14:6-26), Christ said, "I am the way, the truth and the life. No one comes to the Father except through me. If you knew me, you would also know my Father. Already now you know him and see him" (Jn. 14: 6-7). Let us observe, in passing, that *to know* and *to see* have a richer meaning in John's language than an English translation lets us suppose. In the Hebrew idiom, *to know* indicates a very personal relationship with another person. He who knows a person loves him, is closely connected with him and lives with him. *To see* has perhaps still greater depth. It indicates a personal experience of God's presence, a contemplation of His "splendor" and "glory"—words which designate the visible signs in which God's majesty manifests itself to us on earth. In nothing has the Father been made more visible here on earth than in His Son, for the Son *is* the glory of the Father.

Philip, naive and outspoken and always ready to drop remarks, did not understand the Master's words. " 'Lord,' said Philip, 'show us the Father and that will be enough for us.'

'I have been so long with you,' Jesus said to him, 'and you do not know me yet, Philip? He who sees me sees the Father. How do you say: "Show us the Father"? Do you not believe that I am in the Father and that the Father is in me? The words I speak to you, I do not speak from myself; but it is the Father dwelling in me who does his works. Believe me: I am in the Father and the Father is in me. Or else, believe it on account of the works'" (the signs of His living union with the Father as shown by Christ in His miracles). Hereupon follows the assurance that grace, received in faith and thus reaching each one of us personally, brings with it a share in Christ's intimate union with the Father: " 'Indeed, indeed, I say to you, he who believes in me shall himself do the works I do; yes, greater than these shall he do, because I am returning to the Father; and whatever you shall ask in my name, I shall do, in order that the Father may be glorified in the Son.' " This is God's way of letting us see His splendor, His visible divine presence in ourselves.

St. John's narrative goes on. Christ now speaks to His Apostles about their life after His death: " 'If you love me, keep my commandments; and I shall ask the Father, and he will give you another Comforter who is to remain with you forever, the Spirit of truth whom the world is unable to receive because it neither sees him nor knows him. But you know him, because he abides with you and will be in you.' " The presence of the Holy Ghost does not stand in the way of the enduring presence of the risen Lord in our midst: " 'I shall not leave you orphans; I shall return to you. Still a little while, and the world shall see me no more; but you will see me and you, too, will live,' " will share Christ's life.

St. John now summed up these sentences in pregnant words giving us a comprehensive vision of our union with the Father and the Son in the Holy Ghost: " 'In that day you will know that I am in my Father, and you in me, and I in you. He who has my commandments and keeps them, he it is who loves me. He who loves me [the clearest indication of what a life in grace means] will be loved by my Father; and I, too, shall love him, and I shall manifest myself to him.' Judas, not the Iscariot, said to Him: 'Lord, how is it that you will manifest yourself to us and not to the world?' " In the language of St. John, *world* stands for sinful humanity which refuses to believe in Christ and therefore does not keep His commandments, chiefly the commandment of love.

"Jesus answered him: 'If any one love me, he will keep my words; the word which you hear is not mine, but that of the Father who sent me. I told you these things while I was with you. But the Comforter, the Holy Ghost, whom the Father will send in my name, will teach you all things and remind you of all I have said to you.'" A few verses later on comes the telling allegory of the true vine: "'I am the true vine and my Father is the vine-dresser'" (Jn. 15:1). We shall return to this allegory in a moment.

John used no technical theological terms; he used rather what is today called freely existential descriptive forms. Yet once again we notice here what was pointed out before: immanence in the divine Persons and the divine union we possess in both our salvation and the conferring of grace. Each one of the Persons preserves His own proper traits. It is the Father Who sends Christ and, at Christ's request, gives us also the Holy Ghost. It is the Holy Ghost Who will recall all this to our minds and, by doing so, will finish Christ's work in us. It is in Christ, the true vine, that we remain united in grace.

St. Paul's Teaching

St. Paul's writing unfolds the same rich reality before our eyes, but from a different perspective. In his Epistle to the Romans, he tried his best to preserve the Christian message in all its purity against Jewish converts who wanted to impose a Jewish spirituality. In the first seven chapters, he entered the lists against them. He showed the real import of the faith and of justification, the inefficacy of the Jewish Law in relation to salvation, and the dangers inherent in a spirituality based on the Law; and he used the occasion to draw attention to our deep-seated sinfulness. In Chapter 8 (1-17), he called up his own vision of what a Christian life actually is and should be.

For those who are in Christ Jesus there exists no condemnation [or sentence passed on sin]. Through Jesus Christ the law of the Spirit of life has set us free from the law of sin and of death. The [Jewish] Law was powerless to do it because of the flesh [that is, our human sinfulness which that Law could never radically cure]; but God [the Father] has achieved this by sending his Son in the likeness of sinful flesh [in the likeness of man] as a reparation for sin: in the flesh itself [that is, as man] He has condemned sin in order that the justice of the law [holiness of life] be accomplished in us who do not live according to the flesh, but according to the dictates of the Spirit.

Previously we remarked upon the threefold meaning of the word *spirit* in St. Paul. *Spirit* can mean the Person of the Holy Ghost, His gifts, or, more often, the whole man insofar as he is "spiritualized" and completely transformed by the indwelling of the Holy Ghost.

Those who live the life of the flesh [the whole man insofar as he stands under the influence of sin] set their thoughts on sensual things; but those who live the life of the spirit have their minds set on spiritual things. The sensual mind brings only death, but the spiritual mind brings life and peace; for the sensual mind is hostile to God, not submitting itself to God's law; nor can it; they that live according to the flesh cannot please God.

But you do not live the life of the flesh, but the life of the spirit, because the Spirit of God [coming from the Father] dwells in you. If anyone does not possess the Spirit of Christ [Paul spoke first of the Spirit of God and speaks now of the Spirit of Christ], he does not belong to him. If Christ is in you [the presence of the Holy Ghost entails the indwelling of Christ], the body, indeed, may be a thing of death because of sin [that is, it will have to die one day], but the spirit is a living thing [that is, you yourself, insofar as you are filled with the Spirit] because of justification. And if the Spirit of him who raised Christ from the dead dwells in you, he who raised Christ Jesus from the dead [here Paul reverts to the Father] will give life to your mortal bodies, too, through the power of the Spirit who lives in you.

A conclusion follows which sums up existentially, and in suggestive language, what Paul envisaged a Christian life to be: "All those who let themselves be led by the Spirit of God are children of God. The Spirit whom you have received is not, as of old, a spirit of fear ruling you by fear; it is the spirit of adoption which makes us cry: 'Abba!

Father!'" The next verses illustrate well the manifold meaning of *spirit* as used in the New Testament: "The Spirit himself bears witness to our spirit that we are children of God; and if children of God, then also heirs of God and co-heirs with Christ, since we share in his sufferings in order to share in his glorification."

The very fact that in grace and through our living union with the Son we are re-created in His image and likeness gives us an immediate relationship to Him, and this implies an equally immediate presence of the Father and the Holy Ghost. Like the operation at work in the incarnation and redemption, God's action which confers grace upon us is a single divine gesture of love belonging to the three Persons, each exercising His own original and peculiar characteristic.

What is this characteristic, this countenance of the divine Persons? And how does it manifest itself in the operation of grace?

The Countenance of the Father

As an ancient council puts it, the Father is both first and last, "the font and origin of all that is divine." He sends the Son, and together with the Son also sends the Holy Ghost, His Spirit. The Son and the Spirit fulfill Their mission by taking us up into Themselves and together bringing us back to the common wellspring of all being, the Father. The election by grace rests with the Father.

The Father lives in us; He unites us immediately to Himself; for He is the origin and therefore the final goal of the living movement which wells up from God and which carries us back to God in faith, hope and charity—"from God to God," as Ruysbroeck would say:

Mark well with vivid earnestness what it is that we all greatly need. God has, from all eternity, seen and acknowledged us in His Wisdom [the Son]; and He desires that we open our interior eyes and look at Him without reserve. From all eternity He has called us, and He wants us to keep our interior ears steadily open and to listen to the promptings of His grace. From all eternity He has chosen us, and He wants us to choose Him in preference to all creatures. He loves us and has loved us eternally, and He desires us to love Him eternally in return; this is justice: lover united to the beloved, so that the scales be even and equal.

At this moment the scales stand even and the needle of the balance stands steady. In this comparison of his, Ruysbroeck follows the Western interpretation of justice, which does not fully correspond to the biblical concept.

Love is eternal. It begins in God and reaches our spirit, demanding a return of love. So starts the exercise of love between God and us, like a golden link that has neither beginning nor end. Our love starts in God and is perfected in Him. He gives Himself to our spirit, and we in return give our spirit to Him [so that the scales may stand steady and even]. Thereby we bear in our spirit the image of God; and thus we love from God to God, in God and one with God. We are then wise traders. [Again the simile of the scales: wise traders, who measure the "weight" of their love by the measure of God's love.] For we have given our all in return for His all, and we have and hold our all in His all. Now we are sons, and bear God's image in our spirit, to fulfill the purpose for which we are called [that is, we have been created for the purpose of realizing in ourselves the image of God]. . . . Now we are one with God, without loss or gain [because by living we become what we have been eternally destined to be when God marked us with His seal].[12]

The mystery of the Father reaches still greater depths. His basic characteristic is to be Father to the Son; it is in this unique and intense relationship with the Son that He expresses His own personal trait. He is Father with all the quiet might, the absoluteness, the self-evident intensity with which He contrasts Himself with the Son in the one divine nature, never ceasing to possess with the Son the identical divine substance. He never ceases to be completely Himself in His fatherhood vis-à-vis the equally intense Self of the Son. The more He is Himself in His fatherhood, the more He and the Son live in each other and share in the wealth of Their common divinity.

He keeps His fatherhood while conferring grace upon us.

12 Ruysbroeck, *Vanden XII Beghinen*, pp. 169-171.

It is He Who, by granting us His presence through grace, makes us His children. In other words, His active presence is no *abstract* thing. He gives Himself to us *as He is eternally*, that is, as Father and in fatherhood.

"Did God ever say to one of the angels: You are my son, this day I have begotten you? Or again: I shall be a father to him and he will be my son?" (Heb. 1:5). In the loving converse between Father and Son, in the birth of the Son from the Father, each possesses His own proper density of Person. In the same paternal word of grace and mercy, by which He begets us as sons in the Son, not by nature but by adoption, we receive freely and without merit on our part the new density of our re-created personality. The paternal gesture is one: it inclines the Father to the Son, and stretches out to us from all eternity and in accordance with the inner law of life proper to the divine being. Thus it is that the Father raises and transforms us into His children in the Son. "Every one who believes that Jesus is the Christ is born of God," wrote St. John, "and every one who loves the parent who [from all eternity and still now] begets [him], loves also him who is begotten by him," that is, the Son and us all in Him (I Jn. 5:1).

With his gaze on that vision, Ruysbroeck elaborated the whole of his mystical doctrine. No one has shown so vigorously as he that all reality rests basically on the life of the Trinity. It would take us too far afield to try to give a glimpse of what Ruysbroeck has to tell us about the divine image in us, the ultimate foundation of the mystical life of grace. We shall restrict ourselves to a few brief quotations in which the Father's relations to us in the Son are sketched in outline:

God's work is God's Son Whom the Father begets in our spirit.[13]

There [in our innermost self] we are, through love, bent back upon our origin; there we hear the Father's voice which draws us and reaches us [that is, unites Himself immediately to us]; for in His eternal Word, He says to all His elect: "This is My beloved Son, in whom I am well pleased." [14]

For the Father has willingly won us [that is, begotten

---

13 Ruysbroeck, *Vanden Blinckenden Steen*, p. 35.
14 *Ibid.*, pp. 38-39.

us], and He has chosen us in His Son. And because of this, we are gods by grace, though not by nature.[15]

The Countenance of the Spirit

We will now seek to form an idea of how, in the conferring of grace, the Holy Ghost brings into play and at the same time infuses His personal characteristic. This property cannot be easily described. The personal property of the Holy Ghost in its divine fullness transcends our conceptual powers, just as does the relationship between the Father and the Son. In my view, however, theologians embroil their speculative search because they generally confine their attempt to a purely philosophical analysis of the operation of love.

The Western theological tradition has recognized the love of the Father and the Son in the Holy Ghost. Let us accept this as a first orientation in the inner mystery of the Spirit. Most theologians proceed no farther. They pass on at once to subtle analyses of the dynamism of love, a procedure which perhaps befogs rather than clarifies the mystery.

Holy Writ tells us many other truths about the Holy Ghost. These do not resolve the mystery, of course; nevertheless, they prove to be more illuminating than pure philosophical speculation. We shall have to be brief, contenting ourselves with indicating how we catch a glimpse of the Spirit's own countenance in the light of Scripture. After that, we shall appeal to the mystical experiences of Blessed Jan van Ruysbroeck.

The Holy Ghost revealed Himself in the early years of the Church; He let Himself be known as the gift of both the risen Lord and the Father, and often in a pragmatic, miraculous manner. This unique experience of the primitive Church was set down in Scripture; it forms a first attempt at theology. Luke and John are more precise in this respect than any other sacred writers.

To an attentive reader, it is striking how the *working out* of Christ's task, from the moment of the incarnation till the

[15] Ruysbroeck, *Spieghel der Eeuwigher Salicheit*, p. 212.

death on the cross and the resurrection, is attributed to the
intervention of the Holy Ghost.

As early as the Book of Consolation, we are told that
the Servant of Yahweh will announce justice to the nations
and "through his sufferings will bring justice to many"
(Is. 53:11), because God "has placed his spirit on him"
(Is. 42:1). "The spirit of Yahweh, the Lord, is upon me, because Yahweh has anointed me. He has sent me to bring
the good tidings to the poor" (Is. 61:1). When John the
Baptist, then a prisoner of Herod, sent his disciples to Jesus
to ask whether "he is the one who is to come," Jesus answered by quoting the words of Isaias referred to just now
(Mt. 11:2-6; Lk. 7:18-23). At Nazareth, on the day that
Christ came forward in the synagogue and for the first time
spoke publicly of His mission, He cited the Book of Isaias
once more before the assembled village: "This passage of
Scripture, which you have heard just now, is being fulfilled
today" (Lk. 4:21).

At the moment of Jesus' baptism in the Jordan, the voice
of the Father was heard (Lk. 3:22; Mk. 1:11; Jn. 1:32), and
the message of baptism was delivered. The Spirit neither
spoke nor acted in any apparent manner; yet He was present
under the appearance of a dove, a symbol which probably
points to the nature of Christ's mission rather than to Himself. But in that silent presence, so proper to Him, He
caused the meeting of Father and Son to be brought to its
perfection and completion.

Christ acted, prayed, worked His miracles and preached
in the Spirit: "He, who is sent by God, speaks God's own
words; for he gives his Spirit without measure" (Jn. 3:34).
Christ did not experience the Spirit as a foreign power, as
had the prophets of old and as would the apostles later. The
Spirit of truth "will glorify me; for he shall announce to
you whatever he has received from me; for all that the Father has is mine" (Jn. 16:14-15). The Spirit was to be separated neither from the mission sent by the Father nor from
the work of the Son; and yet He remained His original divine
Self, giving reality to and completing the mission and work.
He did this by uniting the *interior* of the Christ-Man more
intimately with the Father and by actuating Christ's *external*
actions in carrying out His messianic and prophetic function.

What the Spirit did for Christ, He did for the Church as
well. The manner of His action was visible and experiential

during the years of the Church's infancy. And it is worth noticing that those years were also the period chosen by the Spirit to reveal Himself as a Person.

It was indeed necessary for Christ to "go away" so that the Spirit might reveal Himself (Jn. 7:39; 16:7). For the Spirit was the "promise of the Father," the gift left to the Church by the dying (Jn. 19:30) and the risen Lord. Everywhere we observe discreetness to be the distinctive mark of the Spirit's operation. The task entrusted to Him does not, in fact, differ from that of Christ; it consists in bringing the work done by the Son in the Father's name to its perfection. "He shall not speak from Himself [that is, in His own name]; but whatever he shall hear [from the Son and the Father] he shall speak, and he shall announce to you the events that are to happen" (Jn. 16:13). The Master had said the same thing elsewhere in other terms: "I am telling you these things while I am still with you. But the Comforter, the Holy Ghost, whom the Father will send in my name, he will teach you all things, and will recall to your mind all I have told you" (Jn. 14:25-26).

Christ's prophecy was accomplished primarily on the day the Church was founded on the first Pentecost, in a specific place, the Cenacle, and at a certain date of our history (Acts 2:1-47). In many respects, the miraculous descent of the Holy Ghost resembles the ratification on Mount Sinai of the choice of Israel as God's people. On both days, we observe the "glory" of the Lord manifesting itself in thunder and lightning; the twelve Apostles represented the twelve tribes of the new Israel, and were granted the gift of tongues, that is, an ecstatic speech in which each listener heard his own tongue. In all this, the living unity of the Church in the Spirit is signified, in opposition to the confusion of tongues and the division of mankind caused by sin and symbolized by the Tower of Babel.

No less significant is the "Pentecost of the Gentiles." In the presence of Peter, the chief witness, the Holy Ghost came down upon the pagan Cornelius and his household (Acts 10-11). Peter would testify on three different occasions "that these men, like ourselves, have received the Holy Ghost, just as He came upon us at the beginning" (Acts 10:47; 11:15-17; 15:8-9). Peter was fully aware of the far-reaching consequences of this exceptional occurrence: "I do now realize, indeed, that God is no respecter of persons, but that, on the contrary, anyone of any nation, who fears him and acts justly, is acceptable to him. He sent the word to the sons of Israel when he proclaimed the good tiding of peace through Jesus Christ who is the Lord of all" (Acts 10:34-36).

While thus manifesting Himself, the Holy Ghost unveiled His own countenance, His divine Self. We are given a description of it mainly in the Acts of the Apostles, a book that has been aptly called the Gospel of the Holy Ghost. Exegetes are agreed in acknowledging that the chief message of Acts lies in showing how the Spirit confirmed the Church, urging her to go forth as an apostolic witness and in that capacity to conquer the world (Acts 1:8, indicating the main theme of the book).

In Acts, St. Luke did more still: he marked another fruit of the "gift of the Holy Ghost," namely, the interior consolidation of the faith in the practice of common prayer, and the reinforcing of the inner surrender to God. He first indicated each new step taken by the nascent Church, and then summed up the significance of her growth by portraying the progress of the Christian community (Acts 2:42-47; 4:32-35; 5:12-16; 9:11; 13:48-52). He underlined each instance of the union and unanimity of the brethren, as these were manifested in their practice of pooling their earthly goods, their joys and their faith. All this, in the mind of Luke, was the fruit of the Holy Ghost.

Paul and John stressed still more the interior consolidation of the faith, and marked how the interior surrender of the brethren, individually and as a society, grew increasingly in perfection.

The "newness of the Spirit" (Rom. 7:6) and the interior "law of the Spirit of life" (Rom. 8:1) stabilize us in our deep, interior liberty as children of God. Only in the Spirit can we truly pray to the Father: "Abba! Father!" (Rom. 8:15-16; Gal. 4:6-7); only in Him are we able to believe that Christ is the redeemer (I Cor. 12:1-3). Only He endows us with true Christian wisdom and empowers the "spiritual man," the man entirely filled with the Spirit, to acquire the "mind of Christ" (I Cor. 2:10-16). The noblest outcome of the life of grace, love coming from God, is reserved to the action of the Spirit: " . . . because the love of God has been poured into our hearts through the Holy Ghost who was given to us" (Rom. 5:5).

The word *pneuma* in the New Testament is the nearest equivalent to what today is called *created grace*. *Pneuma*, or spirit, stands for the whole man when he is totally renewed by the gift of the Spirit. For he then ceases to be "natural man" (I Cor. 2:14), that is, "flesh," and is recreated in a new life, a "renewal of the creature" (II Cor. 5:17; Gal. 6:15).

The Spirit as Gift

Taking a broad view of these elements, we recognize them as various aspects of the operation of grace. They are stamped with the same divine individuality that characterizes the work of the Spirit in Christ: an interior confirmation of the heart in its growing surrender to God, and an exterior radiation of the indwelling divinity in prophetic witnessing. And if that is so, we are entitled to think that the peculiar nature of the Spirit's operation in our life is a distant reflection of the very personal property which He possesses as His own within the Trinity.

He could not but set the seal of His personality on the mission entrusted to Him by the Father and the Son. His mission is to bring the Father's mandate, in the work of the Son, to perfection, to its full existential realization, in each man. And He does this in a twofold movement: first, an *inward movement,* linking all members of the mystical body, in their faith and charity, into one living unit with each other and with God; and second, an *outward movement,* radiating the Christian message in the apostolate. These two movements are inseparable from each other: the first expresses itself spontaneously in the second, while the second keeps the first actual and genuine.

If we want to describe what is proper to the Spirit and to recognize His divine countenance in the faith, we must attempt to discern His personal characteristic in the operation of grace. Relying on his own mystical experience, Ruysbroeck ventured upon the bold step leading from the visible signs of the Spirit's earthly mission to His hidden mysterious Self within the Trinity.

Ruysbroeck knew, of course, the Augustinian tradition which teaches that the Spirit is the "bond of love" between Father and Son, but he was not fully satisfied with it. He preferred to look upon the Spirit as the principle of unity manifested in the ebb and flow of the trinitarian life: "There we have the Father, together with the Son and with all the beloved, surrounded and embraced in the bond of love: and that is the 'unity' of the Holy Ghost. It is the same 'unity' which is at work in the outflow [that is, the procession] of the Persons and remains so in the return flow of the divine life: it remains a bond of love that can never be undone." [16]

The following passage gives a deeper insight into the life of the Trinity:

The nature of the Persons is fecund, eternally at work after the manner of the Persons. For the Father begets the Son, as another issuing from His nature; and the Son is born of the Father, as God's eternal Wisdom, another in Person, but one in nature with the Father. Father and Son pour out from Themselves the Holy Ghost, who is one in nature with Them both. Thus there is oneness in nature and distinction in Persons. For in the common relations between the Persons, there is reciprocal knowledge and love, flux and reflux between the Father and the Son in the Holy Ghost Who is Their common love. But the unity of the Holy Ghost, wherein the Persons live and reign, is active and fruitful [also] in the outward flow making [creating] all things in free liberality [the Spirit], in wisdom [the Son] and in power [the Father]—three properties belonging to the Persons. But in the return flow between the Persons, the unity of the Holy Ghost is the delight which attracts and envelops the Persons, above all distinction, in the bliss of an unfathomable love, which is God Himself in being and nature. [17]

What constitutes the personal property of the Holy Ghost within the trinitarian life should leave its mark on the gifts He bestows on us in our union with the Blessed Trinity: "The Spirit of God is an eternal operation outwards; and He desires that we, too, should work eternally and so resemble Him. But He is also [mystical] repose and [mystical] fruition in the unity of the Father and of the Son and of all His beloved in an eternal rest." [18]

No wonder Ruysbroeck placed human spiritual perfection

16 Jan van Ruysbroeck, *Boecsken der Verclaringhe* (*The Little Book of Enlightenment*), in *Werken*, III, p. 291.

17 Ruysbroeck, *Vanden XII Beghinen*, p. 71.

18 Jan van Ruysbroeck, *Vanden VII Trappen*, tr. F. Sherwood Taylor as *The Seven Steps of the Ladder of Spiritual Love* (Westminster [England]: Dacre), p. 52.

in a state of tension, which both carries and bears up the interior life, between action and contemplation, exterior work and interior repose in the delights of God; for in this precisely lies the image of the personality of the Holy Ghost left by Him in our lives.

The united man [that is, the perfect man] must live for God with the totality of himself, so that he is surrendered to the grace and motion of God, and is docile in all virtues and spiritual practices. In love, he must be raised up and for God die to himself and to all his works, so that he may withdraw [from himself] with all his strength and achieve his transformation into the inconceivable truth which is God Himself. Doing so, he will live by progressing in all virtues, and he will die by entering into God. The perfection of his life lies in these two movements; and these two movements are joined to each other in him as matter and form, as soul and body.[19]

In his concise conclusion, our author associated the riches of such a life with the Holy Ghost: "Because he [the perfect man] maintains and exercises himself in the presence of God, love grows in power in every way." [20]

Ruysbroeck returned to this matter more than once at the end of his book *Seven Steps of the Ladder of Spiritual Love,* and he proposed it as a faithful summary of his spiritual teaching:

And so, to go inwards into the quiescent [mystical] fruition and to go outwards to good works, but ever to remain united to the Spirit of God: that is what I mean. For, as we open the eyes of our body, look and close them again so quickly that we are not aware of it, so we die in God and live from God and remain always one with God. Similarly, we shall go outwards into the activity of the life of sense, and go inwards in love, to cleave to God and remain motionless united to God. Mark well: that is the noblest experience we can perceive and understand in our spirit. We must, however, always go up and down the steps of our heavenly ladder in the practice of interior virtues and exterior

[19] Ruysbroeck, *Boecksen der Verclaringhe,* p. 282.
[20] *Ibid.,* p. 283.

good works, in conformity with the commandments of God
and the precepts of the Church.[21]

The Indwelling of the Blessed Trinity

We are now in a position to sum up the last two sections.
Many a reader brought up on the "classical" theory of grace
—a theory mostly confined to theological circles in the Latin
Church these last three centuries—has gathered from the
preceding pages the somewhat uncomfortable impression that
we are wandering far from the subject matter. Let me assure
him that we are right in the heart of the matter; this will
become plain as we go along.

Essentially, grace consists in this: that God, the Blessed
Trinity, loves us. The trinitarian love consists in the union
of the Father, Son and Holy Ghost with us; or better, Their
drawing us into the intimacy of Their own trinitarian life
by uniting us with Themselves.

In conformity with the language of Scripture, this union
is generally called the divine indwelling. We have called it
also the mystery of God's presence. God's active, transforming union in love imprints the divine image on us; and
here the well-known dictum holds good: *"Amicitia pares
invenit aut facit"* ("Friendship is either found among equals
or it makes equals of those it finds"). The notion of *divine
image* is just another approach to the basic conception of
grace, which is that we share in the divine life. "Whatever
is necessary to life and piety, the divine power has bestowed
on us, together with the knowledge of him who called
us by his glory and virtue. He has granted us thereby his
high and precious promises, so that, leaving behind the corruption of this world with all its evil passions, we may share
in the divine nature" (II Pt. 1:3-4).

All these various conceptions—divine love, presence, indwelling, image and likeness, sanctification and justification
—are simply different approaches through different sym-
bolisms to one identical reality: that through grace we share
in the divine life.

As long as we abide on earth, our share in the divine life
remains hidden; it is a pledge, a foretaste, a seed, a begin-

21 Ruysbroeck, *The Seven Steps* . . . , pp. 60-61.

ning, an anticipation of the life of heaven. But what in fact we already are now will then be made manifest—totally visible, clearly and explicitly experienced, and fully and existentially realized. Heaven is the unveiling of what we already are in and through grace.

A theological inquiry into this participation in the divine nature should not start from abstract notions concerning the divine essence and its attributes. For such a participation is eminently a personal encounter. That is the reason we prefer to explain grace as a presence of one person to another. And that was the deeper sense of our first parable.

In grace we first encounter Christ, the one mediator. It is His image which is imprinted on us; He is the prototype of creation and of the whole order of grace. We have described this image in terms borrowed from Scripture. To encounter Christ signifies that we become servants in the Servant, sons with the Son. Our status as servants in the Servant means that our fallen nature is restored to its original dignity, and that therefore the wounds caused by sin are healed. Theologians designate this aspect of grace by the name *gratia sanans,* healing grace. Our position as sons with the Son indicates rather what in theology is called the elevating aspect of grace. It concretely characterizes the *super*natural character of grace. For such an intimacy with the Father and the Son in the power of the Holy Ghost lies outside the range of any merit of ours; it totally transcends mere human possibility.

Such is the image of God imprinted on us when through grace we are united with the Son, encounter Him in the Church and in the sacraments and thus share in His filial life.

The immediate union with the Son brings with it a union with the Father and with the Holy Ghost; both these unions are likewise immediate, and both bear the mark of the characteristic property of the respective divine Persons.

The origin of all grace can be traced to the election by the Father. To Him belongs the initiative in granting grace. And as the prime cause He is also the ultimate end; we are called to the Father as the final goal of all grace. He calls us to Himself through grace by adopting us as His children, by uniting us with His Son, by extending the inner trinitarian relationship of fatherhood to us wherever we are—or better, by assuming us as adopted children into His relations of love with His Son. He speaks to us in His Son. His divine

"I," which from all eternity utters to His Son a loving "Thou," is addressed to us as well; He raises us and unites us with His Son, saying, "You are my well-beloved sons." And this precisely is the life of grace.

The Holy Ghost, too, dwells in us. He was at work in Christ, and revealed His action and Himself in the primitive Church. He now extends His operation to us, with the same "discreetness" but also with the same intense motive power. Ruysbroeck often mentions the "drive" or "urge" of the Holy Ghost.

The Holy Ghost reveals His own personality in us. It is through the power of the Holy Ghost that the Father impresses the image of the Son on us. In His role as the Spirit of the Father and the Son, He existentially actualizes this image and carries it to the perfection and fulfillment of a personal acceptance. This He does in a twofold manner. First, inwardly He moves us, joined with the Son, to union with the Father in an upward filial surrender, directing us to the Father and "driving" us on in faith, hope and charity. Second, He simultaneously animates us to display outwardly a complete "obedience to the faith" by our Christian witnessing.

As was the case with Christ and is still the case with the Church, the Holy Ghost is the one in Whom our individual encounter with the divine Persons finds its completion, its intimate and existential acceptance and realization, its necessary "commitment." In Him the Father's love reaches its full and authentic expression, making us into the likeness of the Son. It is He Who, strictly speaking, is love. For according to St. John, God, that is, the Father, is love. Nonetheless, the Spirit is the "bond of love," the divine amen to the primordial gesture of love which the Father makes in the Son.

It will help here, by way of conclusion, to quote a powerful passage from the ending of Ruysbroeck's *Seven Steps of the Ladder of Divine Love*:

[On the seventh step] the law of love is fulfilled and all virtues are made perfect. There we are quiescent [in the mystical experience of God]; and our heavenly Father dwells in us with the fullness of His graces, and we dwell in Him beyond all our works and [mystical] delight. Christ Jesus dwells in us and we in Him. In His life we overcome the world and all its sins. With Him, we are raised up in love to our heavenly Father. The Holy Ghost works in us, and we, together with Him, perform all our good deeds. He cries in us with a loud voice and yet without words: *Love the Love which loves you eternally.* His cry is an interior contact with our spirit. His voice is more terrifying than thunder. The lightnings that break from it open up heaven to us and show us the Light and eternal Truth. The heat of His contact and love is so great that it would burn us up. His contact with our spirit cries without ceasing: *Repay your debt! Love the Love which loves you eternally.* With this comes a great impatience, a formless, unstudied conduct; if we repay more than our love demands, we incur still greater debts. Love is never silent; without ceasing, it keeps crying: *Love the Love.* And this is a conflict quite unknown to uninitiated minds.[22]

This tradition has lived on among our people. It may not have often soared to the heights reached by Ruysbroeck and Sister Hadewych, but it has been there, as authentic as life. Let all we have said be one more warning that we are not very interested in subtle speculations, but that we want to propose an undiluted form of Christianity, such as has, in fact, yielded ripe fruits among our people over the centuries. We want to deal with matters of life, of true life.

Redemption, Grace and the Church

Before we pass on to considering created grace, conferred on us by the divine indwelling, we should free ourselves once and for all from individualistic conceptions. We do not say "personalistic," for that is quite another thing. God's indwelling produces a true solidarity in us, one which achieves its living expression in God's people, the Church, the body of Christ, His Bride in heaven and on earth. First, we shall listen to Scripture in order to familiarize ourselves with its spirit. Second, we shall try to work out these same truths

[22] *Ibid.*, pp. 59-60.

more systematically. Our attempt should produce a unified vision of the Church and grace, two inseparable aspects of the redemption. This chapter is of capital importance. The few practical applications which we shall suggest as we go along will provide proof of the depths which these truths can reach in our lives, if they are considered unflinchingly.

Person and Community

Influenced by an atmosphere of dominant individualism, the theology and preaching of recent centuries presented grace all too frequently as no more than an enriching of the individual life of the soul. This, of course, is not accurate. No grace, be it the most intimate, the most exalted mystical gift, is given as a *private* possession. Grace can never be a "thing possessed," simply because it is a life unceasingly flowing out from God and returning to God. Every and all grace is given *in the Church and for the benefit of the Church,* to benefit both the individual receiving it and the community.

If need be, such a view could be vindicated on purely philosophical grounds. Face to face with God, we never stand alone, but together with all other men. God made mankind as one family, and He always sees us as one family. Sin results in division and solitude. It is the role of grace to restore and consolidate the natural unity of the human race driven apart by sin.

The same view finds vigorous support today in the study of the human person. Around the 1920s those who wanted to be up to date let themselves be carried away by the word *person*, not noticing that *person* was frequently mistaken for *personality*. In the flush of their enthusiasm, many saw in the new concept of *person* nothing more than an enrichment of the individual self; they envisaged mainly a free, unhindered self-development. "To become a person" was more or less synonymous with building up mental acumen, training the will and achieving freedom to follow one's own conceits, fancies or moods. That tendency was most noticeable in art. An artist stood apart from the community. He was a solitary man who, by himself and at heights inaccessible to common mortals, had to strike his own path through life.

Many overlooked the paradox that a person discovers himself as a person in proportion as he renounces himself for the sake of others. Christ had already pointed in that direction when *He* endeavored to unveil the deeper meaning of His death on the cross, speaking by implication for His disciples as well: "Indeed, indeed, I say to you: unless the grain of wheat cast into the soil dies, it remains by itself alone; but if it dies, it bears much fruit. He who loves his life [in Aramaic, the word *life* is equivalent to *self*] loses it; but he who hates his life in this world shall preserve it for life eternal. If anyone wants to serve me, he must follow me; and where I am, there too my servant shall be" (Jn. 12:24-26).

In these words Christ stated a truth that acts as a general law in the life of all men. I can recall from the days of my youth a striking experience. There was a young woman who had chosen a career devoted to art and aesthetics, and was nevertheless fitful, caustic, thoroughly unengaging. When I met her again later on, she was a completely changed woman. She had fully surrendered herself to husband and children, and had thus found herself. Very likely, many factors had entered into this change, but the chief reason for her surprising enrichment was undoubtedly her devotion to her family. Such instances are not found only among women, as if men could stand by themselves. We are all made for each other; we cannot become ourselves without selfless devotion, without esteem from others and for others.

We could appeal to modern psychology, which has discovered that before a newborn baby is capable of recognizing its parents, it requires, even for its bodily welfare, love and affection more than food and hygiene.

But let us go at once to what is highest and noblest in our faith, to what we know about the Blessed Trinity. The Father possesses His Self in His fatherhood; the Son is Son because He is totally turned to the Father. The divine Persons are individually so intensely Themselves just because They are so totally, so radically in each other and for each other. And that seems to be the fundamental law of the person. Fashioned in the image of God, we cannot neglect this law without belittling ourselves. God is love; man is man in proportion as he loves. Should we not say that this is so because a man's existence is inextricably intermeshed with that of others and is spent for others? Man discovers himself the moment he realizes this fundamental setting of his life and conforms his conduct to it.

Solidarity in Love

Let us return to the subject of love. We have mentioned previously that the term *grace,* in its primary meaning, signifies love and fidelity, and therefore solidarity in its highest sense. It signifies love and fidelity toward God and therefore love and fidelity toward man. This ought to be self-evident.

In unambiguous language, Scripture says that no one can follow Christ without love. Scripture confronts us with the startling paradox that love for God reaches its visible manifestation in love for neighbor. We like to read about visions and revelations concerning the hereafter; books on this subject, often quite worthless, seem to fetch the largest sales. In one passage of the Gospels, Christ spoke of the last judgment; but as a rule He carefully avoided whetting human curiosity about such matters. To Peter, who betrayed curiosity about what was to happen to John, the Master replied almost curtly, "What is that to you? You just follow me" (Jn. 21:22). Matthew, however, preserved for us a narrative which we cannot read often enough:

When the Son of Man will come in his glory, accompanied by his angels, he will sit upon the throne of his glory. Before him shall be gathered all the nations; and he will divide them one from another as a shepherd divides the sheep from the goats. He will place the sheep on his right side and the goats on his left.

Then the king will say to those on his right side: "Come, you blessed of my Father, inherit the kingdom prepared for you from the foundation of the world. For I was hungry and you gave me to eat. I was thirsty and you gave me to drink. I was a stranger and you took me home; naked and you clothed me, sick and you cared for me, in prison and you visited me." At this, the just will answer: "When did we see you hungry and feed you? or thirsty and gave you to drink? When did we see you a stranger and took you home? or naked and clothed you? When did we see you sick or in prison and visited you?" And the king will answer them: "Indeed, I say to you, as long as you did so to one of the least of my brethren, you did so to me."

And then he will say to those on His left side: "Go far

from me, you the accursed, into the everlasting fire that was prepared for the devil and his angels: For I was hungry and you did not give me food. I was thirsty and you did not give me drink. I was a stranger and you did not take me home; naked and you did not clothe me, sick and in prison and you did not visit me." They, in their turn, will answer: "Lord, when did we see you hungry, or thirsty, or a stranger, or sick, or in prison and did not minister to you?" Then he will answer them: "Indeed, I say to you, as long as you did not do so to one of the least of my brethren here, you did not do so to me." And the latter shall go away into everlasting punishment, and the first ones to eternal life. [Mt. 25:31-46]

Comment seems superfluous. Yet we must admit that it is hard to live up sincerely to Christ's teaching. In case the text of Matthew is not explicit enough, there is also St. John's first Epistle. For John, the supreme characteristic of God the Father is love. This love has come down to us on earth in Christ. And here a surprise awaits us: with all the realism of the mystic, John did not conclude that we have to love God; he concluded that we must love one another. Love for God is apt to conceal many illusions, since we do not see God. The visible, tangible expression of our love for God is brotherly love, the sacrament of our love for God: "Love consists in this: not that we loved God, but that he loved us, and sent his Son to be an atonement for our sins. Beloved, if God so loved us, we too ought to love one another. No one has ever seen God; but if we love one another, then God dwells in us, and the love of God has reached its full growth in our lives" (I Jn. 4:10-12). Farther on, John said, "If anyone boasts of loving God and yet hates his brother, he is a liar. For he who does not love his own brother whom he sees, cannot love God whom he does not see. We have this commandment from him: he who loves God must love his brother as well" (I Jn. 4:20-21). In the eyes of God, every interior disposition should be expressed in humanly visible terms. In this we are given to understand that the Church and grace go together.

The following text in John's first Epistle takes us right to the heart of the problem: "Everyone who believes that Jesus is the Christ, is born of God; and everyone who loves the parent [the Father] loves also the one born of him. If we love God and keep his commandments, we are sure of loving his children. For in this consists the love of God, that we keep his commandments" (I Jn. 5:1-3).

How can we love God if we do not love God's children? It is clear from this alone that grace supposes and confirms a deep-seated solidarity among men. One might even say that this solidarity is given the place of honor in Scripture.

As is well known, the promises made to Abraham had been given in the old covenant to the nation, not to the individuals. The covenant, solemnly sealed on Mount Sinai, bound the Hebrews together into the chosen people of Yahweh. Prophets like Isaias and Ezechiel would later stress the personal responsibility of each individual within the chosen people. Still later, after the exile and a few centuries before Christ, it would be the Law which bound the people together. And so the rabbis would look upon the Law as God's outstanding gift to His people. This legal piety, which found its noblest expression in the strict observance of the Law, implied that each member of the Jewish people considered himself personally responsible for the keeping of the Law. Hence arose the sect of the Pharisees. Their first aim was good, and we can see in the Gospels that there were still some pious Pharisees among the contemporaries of our Lord. It remains always true what St. John repeated so often: the one, true love of God consists in the observance of His holy Law.

Unfortunately, the spirituality of some in the sect grew infected with nationalism and pride. The ideal was to become "a just man." That is precisely the reason the term keeps recurring in the New Testament, in order to bring out the true nature of justice. Among the Pharisees, however, some had persuaded themselves that, relying *exclusively on their own efforts,* they could observe the countless ritual and other laws which the learned rabbis had woven into God's Law. They despised the nations to whom the Law had not been given. What is worse, they despised the Jews not of their sect who, for social or economic reasons or because they were compelled (as in Galilee) to live in the midst of pagans, were not able to live up to the strict letter of the Law. It is on that score that these Pharisees, who should have led their sect to religious excellence, were so mercilessly condemned by Christ in the Gospels and so vigorously impugned by Paul in the Epistles to the Romans and Galatians.

Christ's attitude brings a serious warning home to us.

Christ was God made visible on earth. Now, it is plain from the Gospels that the severe words in which He uttered and therefore revealed God's wrath were not directed against the men whom we priests like to inveigh against, but rather against the pious folk who by their pride denied the true nature of religion. The pride of these Pharisees stood in opposition to God as much as to men. Their sectarianism denied the true solidarity within Israel.

Grace as God's Kingdom

But let us return to the theme of solidarity in Christ, the true brotherhood which grace established in us. We have seen how this brotherhood was prepared in the Old Testament, and how certain rabbis and Pharisees deprived it of all meaning. Herein lay the Jewish betrayal in the days of Christ.

Christ came to extend brotherhood through grace. Solidarity was already a grace because it was a noble gift made by the Father. Christ would stress and emphasize our communion in and with Him. But let us ask ourselves; what did Christ preach? Grace? Not grace directly; He preached the *Kingdom*.

The Kingdom is the object of the *Eu-aggelion*, the Good Tidings. The Kingdom of God is said to be present already, but it has still to grow, like a tree in which birds from all over the world may nest. Only at the end of time will it stand fully revealed.

The Kingdom of God primarily gathers together the Jews, the members of the chosen people; but it is also thrown open to all nations. It is God's highest gift, His highest grace. After the death and resurrection of Christ, the Kingdom found its first realization and visible materialization in the Church, the new chosen people, symbolized by the twelve Apostles who, like the twelve patriarchs of old, form the foundation upon which the Kingdom is built here on earth. Within that Kingdom we all have our home. There and there only shall we encounter God in humility, faith and love.

We should like to emphasize here that the notion of the Kingdom of God finds its best elucidation in what we spoke of above: the presence of the Father in the Son by the power of the Holy Ghost. That is the way in which God exercises His kingship. The notion of the Kingdom adds an important trait to our previous considerations: the divine indwelling assembles us all together into one Kingdom. The Kingdom is both invisible, in that God establishes it, and visible, in that it takes shape here on earth. Through grace we are all children of the Kingdom, and thus we all belong to the visible "people of God on earth," or the Church.

God Acquires a People

The Apostles linked the image of "God's people on earth," or the chosen people of the new covenant, with the central idea of redemption in Christ. We in turn can now purify our idea of redemption and recognize that it is undivided from the doctrine of grace and the Church.

Influenced by ancient Germanic thought and customs about the freeing of serfs and slaves and about the blood money one tribe paid another in the case of manslaughter, the theology of the early Middle Ages built up a theory of redemption which has weighed heavily upon our spirituality to this day. Admittedly, the influence of ancient Germanic times is accidental. We have to look deeper for the real cause. Everyone knows of the law in use among the Jews: an eye for an eye and a tooth for a tooth. Similar customs can be observed among certain tribes in Africa: murder, whether premeditated or not, can be atoned for only by the blood of a member of the tribe that is considered guilty of the murder. Even in fights among children that strange law is observed; a blow can be made up for only by a like blow in return.

This principle of retribution seems to be so widespread that a few theologians have ranked it as a "cosmic law," a universal law of ethics prescribing that amends must be made for every sin by a proportionate measure of pain and suffering. As such, it would apply also to the divine order, the violations by sin demanding reparation. Only one more step was needed in the application of this law to conclude that Christ, by the infinite value of His passion, atoned for the infinite injury done by sin to the divine majesty. Of course, we could not think of denying that Christ offered satisfaction for our sins to the Father, for that is the explicit teaching of both Scripture and the Church. But we may well ask: what does Christ's reparation and satisfaction essentially consist of? Of his love and obedience, shown in His passion and death, or of the weight of His sufferings?

Our question is not a senseless one, for quantitative and juridical conceptions have crept into the theology of penance, confession, indulgences, and even our devotion to the Sacred Heart. On the religious level, human nature is inclined to seek for what is quantitative and mechanical. Quantitative measures are easy to imagine, and would dispense us from personal commitment and self-surrender. But such are not the ways of speaking in Scripture.

There is no denying that in Scripture we come across words like *redeem, ransom,* and even the commonplace phrase *to buy on the market;* but these expressions are given spiritualized meanings in the theology of Scripture. In essence, Christ's redeeming action lies in this: that the Father has acquired a new people in Christ by the power of the Holy Ghost. Consequently, the redemption is conceived by the evangelists, particularly Paul and John, as a deliverance from sin, but still more as a divine action of taking possession—in the vocabulary of the Old Testament, an action by which God's sovereign power takes possession of a people, makes it His very own and gathers it to Himself. This sense holds good in respect both to immediate deliverance from sin through grace and to ultimate fulfillment in heaven, since it is only in heaven that we shall be fully free from sin, totally belonging to God, definitively accepted into His Kingdom.

In this light, the authentic teaching of Scripture assumes great power. Christ's redeeming action is not restricted to the cross alone; the death on the cross is inseparably bound up with the resurrection and the ascension. Like the Jews of the Old Testament, we celebrate the feast of our deliverance on Easter day, not exclusively on Good Friday. Our deliverance is signified in both the death and the resurrection of Christ, and consequently has been accomplished in them both. The resurrection is not just an adjunct, as we have sometimes heard it stated; it is not simply an apologetical proof that the Man Who died on Good Friday was God. This conception, which is still current in some countries, plainly runs counter to the explicit teaching of Scripture, of the tradition contained in the liturgy and of the great Fathers of the Church. This is the error of a theology which has lost consciousness of its dependence on Scripture and wants to base itself on pure speculation. We have actually heard it contended that, compared to systematically built-up speculation, Scripture is but a primitive, raw and naive interpretation of the faith. Had we not better say that it is the other way round?

Christ, then, did not buy our freedom by the excess of His sufferings, quantitatively measured as an infinite satisfaction, but *through the love and obedience* which animated His passion and death. His love and obedience proved themselves most tellingly on the cross, but they attained their highest achievement in the resurrection.

On this point, no doubt is possible in the writings of John and Paul. Toward the end of Christ's first farewell discourse, John put these words on the Master's lips: ". . . the world must know that I love the Father and that I do as the Father has commanded me. Rise, let us depart from here" (Jn. 14:31). And Christ got up from the table and went to the Garden of Olives. Earlier in the same Gospel, as he was about to begin the story of the passion, John repeated the same idea in most solemn language that leaves no doubt about his true thought: "Jesus, knowing that the hour of his departure from this world to go to the Father had come, and still loving his own who were in the world, gave them the utmost proof of his love" (Jn. 13:1). The solemnity of these words is evidence enough that what was uppermost in St. John's mind was not the episode of the washing of the feet that follows in his text, but the story of the passion taken as a whole. And this is demonstrated still further in verse 3, the tone of which is equally impressive: "Knowing that the Father had given all things into his hands, that he had come from God and was now returning to God, he laid aside his outer garments, took up a towel and put it about him." The repetition of the phrases "to depart from the world to the Father," "to come from the Father," and "to return to the Father" guarantees that John, so fond of playing on words with complex meanings, had the Hebrew term *pascha* in the foreground of his thought. Now, *pascha*, from which we derive the English word *pascal*, signified for the Jews a crossing over, a passage, and especially the crossing of the Red Sea into liberty. In His second farewell discourse after the last supper, Christ suggested the same idea when He said, "This is my commandment, that you love one another as I have loved you. No one has greater love than this: that he should lay down his life for his friends" (Jn. 15:12-13).

In other, broader contexts, John suggested the same order of ideas more than once. For instance, in the narrative of Christ's conversation with Nicodemus, he wrote:

The Son of Man must be lifted up [in another section, we pointed out that "to lift up" refers to the song of the servant of Yahweh in the Book of Consolation, Is. 53:13-15] as Moses of old lifted up the serpent in the desert [another image of deliverance; see Nm. 21:8] in order that anyone who believes in him may have eternal life. For God so loved the world that he gave his only begotten Son, so that anyone who believes in him may not perish, but have eternal life. God did not send his Son into the world to condemn the world, but in order that the world might be saved through him. [Jn. 3:14-17]

In His sacerdotal prayer, Jesus prayed for His own and for all the faithful. Death was imminent; a few paces separated him from the Garden of Olives. And what did Christ expect from the Father? He asked for and expected a union that could be nothing else than a powerful revelation of God's glory:

I do not pray for them alone [the Apostles], but also for those who through their word believe in me, that all may be one, as you, Father, are in me and I in you, that they too may be one in us, in order that the world may believe that you have sent me. I have given them the glory which you have given me, so that they may be one as we are one. I in them and you in me, that they may be made perfectly one, and the world may know that you have sent me and love them as you have loved me. . . . Your name I have revealed to them and will reveal; so that the love with which you have loved me may be in them, and I, too, may be in them. [Jn. 17:20-26]

The visible union of which there is question here undeniably witnesses to the glory of the Father, to His grace. "Glory," in Hebrew usage, refers to the majesty of God insofar as it can be manifested in this world.

John said all this once again in his first Epistle: "He who does not love, does not know God [in Hebrew, not to know God means "not to have true piety"], for God is love. The love of God has been revealed, where we are concerned, by the fact that God has sent his only begotten Son into the world, so that we might have life through him" (Jn. 4:9). This is the way St. John spoke of our redemption—as the visible manifestation of the Father's love in the obedience and love of the Son. Through this love we have received love and have been brought together in a new unity. John went as far as comparing this new unity in grace with the supreme unity existing between the Father and the Son. This is one more illustration of the intimate connection among the three mysteries of grace, redemption and the Church.

Redemption Through Obedience

St. Paul was still clearer, if this is possible. In Christ's death on the cross, he saw the Revelation and the guarantee of God's love for us.

While we were still powerless to help ourselves, Christ, at the fitting time, died for us sinners. It is hard enough to find anyone who will die on behalf of a just man, though there may be one who might contemplate dying for a deserving man. [This is an echo of the Master's words in St. John: "No one has greater love than this: that he should lay down his life for his friends" (Jn. 15:13). In fact, Paul added emphasis to John's text by saying that Christ died for His enemies.] But God proves his love for us in this, that, while we were still sinners, Christ died for us. All the more surely, now that we have been justified through his blood, shall we be saved, through him, from his wrath. Though enemies of God, we were reconciled to God through the death of his Son; and now, reconciled to Him, we are surer than ever of having salvation in his Son's life. [Rom. 5:6-10]

More than once we have referred to the great text from the Epistle to the Philippians which re-echoes so powerfully the consciousness the Church has of her faith. This text keeps recurring in the mass and the breviary during Holy Week and Easter Week. It forms the fundamental theme of the powerful symphony that the pascal celebration ought to be to us; it offers us the true content of the pascal mystery. "Appearing as man, he has humbled himself by being obedient unto death, even to the death of the cross. And therefore, God has lifted him up [image of the Servant of Yahweh] and has bestowed upon him the name above all names . . . Jesus is the Lord" (Phil. 2:8-11).

Because of His obedience, Christ was invested with the very majesty of the Lord, of Adonai. This word was in use among the rabbis to speak of God's supreme title, Yahweh, "the name above all names," which inspired such awe that it was hardly ever pronounced. The same sacred name also conveys the idea of what the kingship of Yahweh is. In Christ, God's Kingdom has been founded and permanently established.

Redemption and Community

St. John contemplated our Christian solidarity in its ultimate source, the Blessed Trinity. Our unity has its origin in the Father, Who is love, light and life. This love, this light and this life have been revealed to us in Christ, and are continually being consolidated by His Spirit. There we discover the root and ground of our *koinonia*, our communion with each other. As the Father is one with the Son, so are we one with the Son and thus with the Father. Our union, consequently, is a share in the inner divine life, in the grace that comes down from God and returns to God.

St. Paul preferred to see that same unity in its visible form, the Church. Yet he did not shrink from looking upon the unity within the Church as issuing from the Trinity. It is precisely in this that the great "mystery" consists, the "mystery" Paul was commissioned to announce to the Gentiles, who once upon a time had been "so far away" and now were "brought close" to Christ.

Remember, therefore, that formerly you were called Gentiles . . . that in those days [before the Gospel was preached to them] you were apart from Christ, outlaws from the commonwealth of Israel, strangers to the covenant of the promise, without hope and without God in the world. But now [in opposition to "formerly"; the time of salvation has come in Christ] in Christ Jesus you, once so far away, have been brought close in the blood of Christ. For he is our peace, who made the two nations one, breaking down

in his flesh [His human nature] the wall that was a barrier
between us, the enmity there was between us. He put an end
to the Law with its decrees [the rabbinic Law caused
division, not unity]. He has made peace, remaking the two
human creatures into one new man in himself, so that he
might reconcile them both in one body to God through his
cross, inflicting death upon the enmity. And he came and
brought the good tidings of peace [and thus of unity] to
you who were far off, as well as to those who were near
[the Jews of the covenant]; for through him we have both
[Jews and Gentiles] access in the same Spirit to God.
[Eph. 2:11-18]

Paul followed this up with the lofty conclusion: "So then,
you are no longer strangers and aliens [that is, people
living in a foreign country]; but you are fellow-citizens with
the saints; you are of God's household, built upon the
foundation of the apostles and the prophets, the chief
corner-stone being Christ himself. In him, the whole building, aptly fitted together, grows into one temple dedicated to
the Lord; in him you [the Gentiles], too, are being built in
and with the others into one dwelling-place of God, in the
Spirit" (Eph. 2:19-22).

There we have the "mystery" which Paul preached. Since
all eternity, it had lain hidden in the secret of God's designs.
It was now revealed in Christ, animated and sealed by the
Spirit. Of all this, Paul was the "Apostle," the one sent to
the Gentiles.

Every one of these themes is enunciated in the opening
chapter of the same Epistle to the Ephesians, which for this
reason has justly been called "an Epistle concerning the nature
of the Church":

Blessed be God, the Father of our Lord Jesus Christ, who
has blessed us in the heavens with every spiritual blessing in
Christ. In Christ, he [the Father] chose us out before
the foundation of the world to be holy and blameless in his
sight. In love, he predestined us to become his children
through Jesus Christ, in accordance with the good pleasure
of his will, to make manifest the splendor of the grace with
which he has favored us in the well-beloved, in whom we
have redemption through his blood, remission of sins, by the
wealth of his grace that has overflowed in us in an abundance
of wisdom and discernment. For He [the Father] made
known to us the hidden purpose of his will, the free design

which He had determined to carry out in the fullness of time: to bring all things in Christ under one head, those that are in the heavens and on earth [all] in him.

In him, we also [the Jews, in opposition to "you" which follows] have obtained our inheritance, chosen beforehand to suit the purpose of him who works out all things according to the design of his will, in order that we might serve to praise his glory, we who were the first to hope in Christ. In him, you too [the Gentiles], after hearing the word of truth, the gospel of your salvation, in him, you too have believed, and have been marked with the seal of promise of the Holy Spirit, who is the pledge of our inheritance until the [full] redemption of those whom God has acquired to the praise of his glory. [Eph. 1:3-14]

The Body of Christ

With these truths as a light and a foundation, Paul built up his theology of the Body of Christ. Let us start by observing that the phrase *Body of Christ* has three meanings in St. Paul. It means, first, the human body of Christ which died and rose for us, and on that account was no longer a "psychic" (natural) body but a "spiritual body" (I Cor. 15:44), a "body of glory" (Phil. 3:22). After that moment, Christ's risen body became the sign of God's presence on earth, and it is now what the temple of Jerusalem was previously for the Jews (Jn. 2:19). In St. Paul, it became the cornerstone of the new temple, which is the Church (I Cor. 3:10-17; II Cor. 6:16-20; Eph. 2:20:22).

Christ's body remains visible in the mystery of the eucharist (I Cor. 11:24). In the celebration of the eucharist, Paul experienced the fact that together we form one body— the Church; and this is the third meaning of the word. "The bread which we break [one of the earliest expressions to designate the eucharistic meal: bread must be broken, as was done by Christ, to be distributed], does it not give a participation of the body of Christ?" Then follows a very ancient symbolism which, unfortunately, we have largely forgotten, though it can be detected in the earliest prayers after communion: "The one bread [one because formed from many grains] makes us one body; for the same one bread is shared by many. Look at Israel of this earth: do not those who eat of their sacrifice associate themselves with the altar of sacrifices?" (I Cor. 10:16-18).

In his Epistles to the Corinthians and the Romans, the Apostle almost surely had in mind the image, rather common in the Greek world of those days, in which the term *body* suggested the solidarity among the multitude of citizens belonging to one city. Each has his individual life and occupation, and yet all hang together. In the first Epistle to the Corinthians (12:12-16), Paul did not hesitate to draw inspiration from a Greek tale about the limbs of the body and the stomach, and apply the image to Christian solidarity.

However, in Paul, the Greek symbolism acquires a deeper significance. First of all, as stated above, we form one Body by partaking of Christ's body in the eucharist. In Chapter 12 of the first Epistle to the Corinthians, we have these words: "Just as the [human] body is one single thing, though it has many members, all the members of the body, though many, are one body"; and the text continues: "So it is with Christ." Notice that Paul did not say, "So it is with the Christians." "In one and the same Spirit, we are all baptized into one body, whether Jews or Greeks, slaves or freemen; and we were all made to drink of one and the same Spirit" (I Cor. 12:12-13). The same principle serves to bring these considerations to their conclusion: "So now, all together you are the body of Christ, and individually members of it" (I Cor. 12:27). The same conclusion appears in the Epistle to the Romans: "We, though many, form one body with Christ, but as individuals, we are members mutually dependent on each other" (Rom. 12:4).

Like John, Paul based this unity in diversity on the living unity of the Blessed Trinity. He first established that we cannot possibly be Christians without the immediate influence of the Holy Ghost: "No one can say, 'Jesus is the Lord' [the earliest Christian profession of faith], unless by the Spirit." He then continued: "There are different kinds of gifts, but it is the same Spirit. And there are different kinds of service, but it is the same Lord [Christ]. And there are different kinds of power [to work wonders], but it is the same God [the Father] who manifests his power in us all." The text sums up the varieties of spiritual gifts granted by the Holy Ghost, and ends: "But all these are the effects of one and the same Spirit, who distributes them to the individuals according as he wills" (I Cor. 12:3-11).

In his later letters, known as the Captivity Epistles, Paul

went one step farther. It is only in these writings that he explicitly described Christ as the head of the Body, and called this Body the Church.

Soon after the opening verses of the Epistle to the Colossians, Paul quoted an ancient hymn to Christ, which we have cited in a previous section:

He is the image of the invisible God, the first-born of all creatures. For in him all things were created, whether in the heavens or on the earth, what is visible or invisible, whether Thrones or Dominations, Principalities or Powers. All things have been created through him and for him. He exists before all things, and in him all things subsist. He is also the head of the body, which is the Church. He is the beginning, the first-born among the dead, so that in all things he may hold pre-eminence; for it has pleased God the Father that in him should dwell the fullness [of the Father], and that, through him, he should reconcile all things to himself, whether the things on earth, or the things in the heavens, making peace by the blood of his cross. [Col. 1:15-20]

This Pauline teaching confronts us with a theology of the Church far more profound than is commonly suspected. Just as Christ possesses in Himself the indwelling fullness of the divinity, so also the Church holds within her the fullness of Christ: "And he [the Father] subjected all things under his feet [that is, under His dominion], and has made him supreme head of the Church, so that the Church is his body, the completion of him who completes all things everywhere" (Eph. 1:22). The cosmic fullness of the Church, grounded in Christ and therefore in the Father, has as its immediate, visible manifestation the fact that all men, even the Gentiles, are called to the Church. In the verses that follow those just cited, the Apostle dealt at some length with this call, as it affected both Jews and Gentiles, and used it to stress once again our common solidarity in Christ.

Paul was well aware that, with this doctrine, he definitively broke away from the general rabbinical teaching which he had learned in his youth, prior to his conversion, at the feet of Gamaliel in Jerusalem. The rabbis generally taught that there were three classes of humans whom God excluded from the blessings of the Law: Greeks (that is, the Gentiles or, as the Old Testament calls them, the nations), slaves and women (though these could share through their husbands in the promises made to Abraham). Seen against this background, the following assertion of Paul in his Epistle to the Galatians stands out in bold relief: "Through faith, you are all sons of God in Jesus Christ. For all of you, by your baptism into Christ, have put on Christ [yet another simile of union with Christ]. Henceforth there is neither Jew nor Gentile, neither slave nor freeman, neither man nor woman: they are all one in Christ Jesus. But if you are Christ's, you are the seed of Abraham, heirs in virtue of the promise" (Gal. 3:26-29). In other words, all without exception would henceforth be members of the new Israel, God's people on earth, the people of the promise, heirs of the Kingdom.

Paul saw the image of Christ's intimate union with His Church realized in a special way in Christian marriage. In the well-known words of Genesis 2:24, the marriage union is expressed in typically Hebrew fashion: "and these two will be one flesh," that is, one man. The Apostle plainly had this text in mind when he spoke of the union of Christ with the Church as the fruit of the redemption:

For the husband is head of the woman, as Christ is head of the Church; now he is the Savior of her who is his body. Well then, as the Church is subjected to Christ, so women are subjected to their husbands in all things. Husbands, love your wives as Christ has loved his Church, and has delivered himself up for her in order to make her holy and pure through the bath of water together with the word [that is, through baptism and faith in the Word], so as to acquire her as a glorious bride, free from stain or wrinkle or anything like it, but holy and undefiled. . . . No one has ever hated his own flesh, but each one has nourished it and cared for it, just as Christ did for the Church, since we are all members of his body. That is why man shall leave father and mother in order to attach himself to his wife; and these two shall be one flesh. This mystery is a great one; I am applying it to Christ and his Church. [Eph. 5:23-32]

Paul did not intend to strain the comparison unduly. Yet he looked upon the intimacy of the marriage union as a replica of the standard for all unions on earth: the union of Christ with His Bride, the union of the head with the Body, the Church. The example of marriage helps us to realize better how deeply we are *all* united to Christ.

For Paul, the Church was never an abstraction, but was rather the sum total of her members. At the same time, this profound truth, the "mystery of salvation" which gives Christian marriage its ultimate meaning, must prompt husbands and wives to love each other as Christ loves the Church and as the Church owes herself to Christ.

Was not Paul justified in proposing union among the faithful as the highest of Christian duties? In the text we cite below, he saw this union as rooted in the Trinity; and he had no difficulty in laying bare the ultimate foundation of our obligation to foster union, peace and love: "Endeavor to maintain the unity of the Spirit in the bond of peace. There is but one body and one Spirit, as you have been called to one hope by your vocation. There is but one Lord [Christ], one baptism [given us by the one Lord]. There is but one God and Father of all, who is above all, acts through all and dwells in all" (Eph. 4:3-6).

Unity in Its Fulfillment

Union is already achieved now; but we must wait until Christ returns at the end of time for its full revelation. This is what St. John tells us, especially in the Book of Revelation, the Apocalypse. In a previous page, we saw how this union signified for John a share in the union of the Son with the Father. While St. Paul developed the metaphor of the body, St. John enlarged upon the image of the vine:

I am the true vine, and my Father is the vine-dresser. Any branch on me that does not bear fruit, he removes; and any branch that bears fruit, he prunes in order that it may bear more fruit. You are pruned already because of the word I have spoken to you. Abide in me, and I will abide in you. As the branch cannot bear fruit unless it remains on the vine, so neither can you, unless you abide in me. I am the vine, you are the branches. He who abides in me, and I in him, he it is who bears much fruit, for apart from me you can do nothing. If someone does not abide in me, he is cut off like a branch and withers; and they will gather them up and throw them into the fire to be burnt up. If you abide in me, and my words abide in you, ask whatever you want and it shall be done to you. In this my Father is glori-

fied that you bear much fruit, and so you will be my disciples.
As the Father has loved me, so have I loved you. Stay in my
love. [Jn. 15:1-9]

The Church is not mentioned explicitly in the metaphor of
the vine. The next to last chapter of the Apocalypse makes
up for this omission. Our union with the Father, Son and
Holy Ghost is fully achieved only in the Church triumphant,
the Bride of the Lamb. In an effort to utter the ineffable
and to describe the glory of heaven, St. John searched the
Old Testament for appropriate symbols: heaven as the
holy city of Jerusalem, God's dwelling among men in the
tabernacle of the covenant; the twelve tribes of Israel and
the twelve Apostles, the image of God's new people; and
finally, an older metaphor of paradise, the stream of living
waters described in the prophecy of Ezechiel (47:6-12) and
designating the Holy Ghost. St. John concluded the narrative
of his heavenly vision by mentioning the Blessed Trinity,
which is the beginning and the end of our redemption, our
grace and the Church.

Then I saw a new heaven and a new earth. . . . I saw the
holy city, the new Jerusalem, coming down out of heaven
from God [as the highest gift and grace], beautiful as a
bride adorned for her husband. And then I heard a mighty
voice proclaiming from the throne [image of God's majesty],
"Now at last, God has his abode among men! He will dwell
among them. They will be his people, and he himself will be
God with them [an ancient expression to denote the covenant between God and men].". . .
Then one of the angels who holds the seven bowls full of
the seven last plagues came to me and said: "Come and I
will show you the Bride of the Lamb." So, in the spirit he
carried me up to a very high mountain, and showed me the
holy city of Jerusalem coming out of heaven from God and
shining with the glory of God. . . . The city was ringed
with a very high wall and twelve gates, at which stood twelve
angels; and on the gates were written the names of the
twelve tribes of Israel. . . . The city wall had twelve foundation stones on which were inscribed the twelve names of
the twelve apostles of the Lamb.
. . . the city was of pure gold, bright as clear glass.
. . . But the temple itself I did not see; for the temple
was the sovereign Lord and the Lamb. [Henceforth we live
in the immediate presence of the Father and the Son.]

And the city had no need of the light of sun or moon; for the glory of God shone upon it; its lamp was the Lamb. . . .

[Now comes the Holy Ghost:] Then the angel showed me the river of the water of life [as in paradise], clear as crystal and flowing from the throne of God and of the Lamb, and running down the middle of the city's street. On either side of the river stood a tree of life, yielding twelve crops of fruit [symbol of abundance], one for each month. The leaves of the trees serve to bring health to the nations.

There will be no longer any profanation in this city. The throne of God and of the Lamb will be there, with his servants to worship him; they shall see him face to face, his name written on their foreheads [as a sign of possession]. There will be no more night, nor will they need the light of lamp or sun; for the Lord God will shed his light upon them; and they shall reign for ever and ever. [Ap. 21:1-22:5]

In this section we have wandered leisurely through the luxuriant garden of Scripture. The first impression may well have been rather confusing. Scripture is no formal French garden, like that at Versailles; it is rather like mountain country with pleasant dales, meadows and woods, and here and there a breathtaking vista, all beneath the splendor of lofty ranges and summits. Scripture is not made up of systematic works in which problems are examined singly and worked out methodically. Scripture contains unorganized writings—letters, for instance—and also some historical books, prepared for the purpose of instruction rather than to supply the reader with scientific history, such as he is used to today.

Repeatedly in this section we have come face to face with the central doctrine outlined in the three preceding sections. The Church is not to be conceived of as apart from the living presence of the Father, the Son and the Holy Ghost. One could write at length about the Church and her diverse aspects. To begin with, she was established by the will of the Father. In being and essence, she is and will always remain the Body of the head, Who is Christ. Since the day of the first Pentecost, she has been borne up all through her historical development by the power of the Holy Ghost. Recent papal documents call the Holy Ghost the soul of the Body; Scripture calls the Church the temple of the Holy Ghost.

The hidden, vital energy which keeps the Church together

and animates her from within is precisely the "living life" of the Blessed Trinity. Now, the Church has no existence apart from her members; she is not a juridical apparatus, or still less an idea hanging in midair. Consequently, whatever applies to the Church is applicable to the members in which she lives—those who are now her members and those who are destined to enter the Church. We should exclude no one. She is the mother of us all in Christ.

Further, we have seen that the great mysteries of our faith—redemption, grace and the Church—are not to be thought of as independent of each other. We have been set free through the obedience and love of the Son, sent by the Father Who is love. The Son walked in our midst in the power of the Spirit, the Spirit of truth and love. The central core of the divine redeeming act lies in this, that the Father took to Himself a people and made it His very own; He sanctified it in Christ through His Spirit, freeing it from sin and filling it with grace. Grace is the fruit of the redemption; but our redemption was not worked out on a quasi-juridical basis, as if Christ's abundant sufferings merited a determined quantity of grace—a notion hard to get hold of, anyhow. Grace must be seen as the natural flowering of Christ's redeeming action. That being so, grace cannot be conceived of as separate from the Church, for both are but aspects of the same reality: salvation.

We shall have occasion to return to this matter. There is perhaps no more urgent task in theology than to purify our ideas on this subject. The creative, renovating presence of the Blessed Trinity has proved itself above all in the redemption. Sent by the Father and filled with the Spirit, Christ entered into human history and became God's obedient Servant and loving Son. In His humanity, He testified to what He, as Son, ever continues to be within the Trinity: totally surrendered to the Father in the love of the Holy Ghost.

In this world of ours, estranged from God by sin, Christ was what we men have been expected to be since the beginning of the world: God's servants as creatures, God's children by grace. And that is the way He chose to redeem us, the one way God thought of and accepted as a fitting expiation and satisfaction. God is no sadist to be appeased by the sufferings of a sinner. Does not a true conversion, a true satisfaction and expiation, consist in a *change of heart*, the *metanoia* Scripture speaks of?—the conversion from disobedience to obedience, from pride and self-love and hate of others to love and self-surrender? To be accurate, we should say that Christ merited for us the possibility of becoming God's obedient servants and loving children with, in and through Him.

Before God, *to merit* has a different and far deeper meaning than what it signifies in human relations. This is pretty obvious, of course, though it is all too often overlooked. Christ's "meriting" for us means that He won for Himself, both as God and as man, the power to let us share in His obedience and love, and at the same time obtained God's pardon for us. The life of grace, as we noted above, is simply this. And because we share in this change of heart, in this obedience and love; because He has gathered all of us around Him and unites us to Him through the power of His Spirit, it ought to be plain that the being and substance of the Church is not to be thought of as distinct from grace. In fact, the Church is grace *par excellence,* insofar as she manifests visibly that aspect of grace which binds us all, like brothers and sisters, into a true and everlasting people of God, the new Israel, the people of the promise and of the inheritance.

Until now we have made no mention in this section of those aspects of the Church with which the catechetical instruction and preaching in vogue today have made us familiar. I mean the Church's *authority,* evidenced in a corpus of law and a fairly extended formal organization. Nor have we ventured to say anything about the Church as a society devoted to religious worship, the prominent acts of which are the offering of the mass and the reception of the sacraments. No harm is done if we shift the emphasis to the Church as a living society, as a *koinonia* which comes alive in a fuller realization of our solidarity and association in destiny, of our true brotherhood in love.

It would be unwarranted to slur over these visible aspects, to push them aside as mere adjuncts or, worse still, to exclude them from the realm of grace. It was fashionable to do so in the nineteenth century, and that fashion has not yet passed. History has known more than one sectarian movement which began with displeasure and embitterment at the blatant abuses displayed in the visible Church, and ended by taking refuge in a purely spiritual conception of what the Church is. Only cowardice flees from reality; and in this instance, cowardice is wrongheadedness to boot. The

Church's founder wanted her to be a visible reality for no other reason than that she belongs to a visible world.

And so, if we have dwelt on the fact that we are one society in Christ, we have not for a moment forgotten that the Church, founded by Christ, is a visible Church. Hence our vigorous insistence on this society's need for practical love between its members in order to grow in actuality. In the Church, some have been commissioned to exercise authority and others to preach or to sanctify by performing visible ritual actions, that is, by administering the sacraments. Episcopal and sacerdotal authority was instituted by Christ when He sent His Apostles on their missions. The sacraments, too, come from Him. For it is the fundamental law of the incarnation and the redemption that God became man so that we might become partakers of the divine life. God leads through the visible to the invisible, that is, to Himself. We cannot proceed better in our discussion than by giving some insight into the meaning of what is visible in the order of grace.

Twofold Movement of Life Within the Church

We may distinguish two movements of life within the Church. The first is one that comes down from God to us, and the second goes up from us to God. Otto Semmelroth has named the first movement the line of initiative and authority proper to the husband, and the second the line of self-surrender proper to the bride. Such figures of speech have a suggestive value and nothing more, though the latter seems to us to be the more felicitous of the two.

Here again we come across the trinitarian formula so familiar to the early Church Fathers and to the liturgy: everything comes to us from the Father through the Son in the Holy Ghost, and everything must return from us through the Holy Ghost in the Son to the Father. With Ruysbroeck, we have applied this hospitable statement to grace. It has the great advantage of preventing our conceptions about God and grace from stiffening into static notions. John and Paul applied the same scheme to the incarnation and redemption; it is thus to be ranked among the oldest theological axioms. Because it is an elaboration of the human mind, it needs to be corrected each time we apply it to God. But it keeps our theological thought "on the move"—which is the main thing.

We shall then distinguish between the Church as Body of Christ in the descending movement and the Church as Bride of Christ in the ascending movement.

The Church as Body

Insofar as the Church, *qua* Body of Christ, remains united to her head, she participates in His messianic and prophetic function. And to do so all the members of the Church, in and with Christ and filled with His Spirit, must bear witness to the truth in the face of the world. We do this principally by living a genuine Christian life. No one may consider himself dispensed from this function. Whether or not this deserves to be called the "apostolate"—an overworked and often misused term—it is the duty of baptized and confirmed Christians, for it is the Holy Ghost Who bears witness in them. He who holds and exercises an ecclesiastical office is under the obligation to observe keenly how the Holy Ghost is operating among the faithful and what He is stirring up among them. It is in this sense that the Church as a whole is infallible in her witnessing, inasmuch as the members, according to their various statuses (some in free obedience, others in authority, though all in unity of faith), are kept within the truth by the Holy Ghost and bear witness to the truth. On this basis, we feel called upon to follow the freedom and boldness which is ours as the voice of the Holy Ghost, in spite of our conscious weakness and sinfulness. However, as no guarantee can be had that His voice is to be heard outside the Church, each one of us is duty bound to test the interior voice by the faith of the whole Church, though no member of the Church is exempted, even for a moment, from the obligation of listening to the voice of the Holy Ghost in his personal life. If this rule were lived up to, it would banish all danger of Christian legalism; it would restore to us all the freedom of the children of God.

The authoritative preaching of the word of God and the management of the society of the faithful have been entrusted to a few members within—and therefore not above —that same society; their ordination is their "sending." The priestly mandate was instituted by Christ when He sent His Apostles on their mission. Of that mission the universal episcopate has taken the lawful and visible succession.

The fact that this mission is realized still further in the form of definite laws and a concrete organization is inseparably linked with Christ's express appointment of these men to be leaders of a visible human society. Through the centuries, these laws and this organization will develop and adapt themselves to new conditions of life or to different cultural traditions; but the substance of Christ's institution must remain intact. Saying this, we have implied that these visible forms are open to reform and adjustment, and the second Vatican Council has brought this out clearly enough. But such as they are, they are no more—or less— than the normally human, historically determined forms in which the religious authority, willed by Christ, takes visible shape. In these manifestations of authority, we acknowledge the visibility of grace coming to us in the Church. We believe this authority to be infallible within certain limits, which simply means that within these limits we have the assurance that Christ, head of the Body, speaks to us through His Spirit.

This is equally clear from the fact that Holy Scripture frequently describes this mission as a form of *diaconia,* a term meaning *ministerium* or service, which has been preserved in some European languages. Priests are indeed the servants of the Church and of the faithful, but above all they are the servants of Christ and of the Spirit. Not for a moment does their authority harden into a personal possession. These men are in the service of grace.

Assuredly, being humans and sinners like ourselves, they may abuse this authority, using it for their own ends. But we firmly believe that Christ's guidance, at work within the Church, will never permit them to debase what belongs to the substance of the message of grace. In other words, the presence of the Blessed Trinity is so sovereignly assured in the ecclesiastical function that the men who are appointed to exercise this function cannot escape from the divine power of grace, whatever their personal sins. We are speaking of the bishops all over the world, in communion with each other and with the See of Peter. History teaches us that priests and bishops, individually or even in numbers, can fall away from God's truth and grace, but that catastrophe overtakes them only when they deliberately take their stand outside the unity of their function. By their sin, they may possibly succeed in shrouding and obscuring the glory of grace, but they are unable to pervert it totally.

Further evidence is had from the duty inherent in the Church's noblest function: her sanctifying mission. In the name of Christ, the Church sanctifies by administering the sacraments, which are all centered upon the eucharist.

This sacramental duty, more than any other role, highlights in strong relief the Church's inner nature as Body of Christ and her function in the service of grace. The priest or bishop is the ordinary minister of most sacraments (today, some theologians would say that even the sacrament of marriage is no exception). And in the *present order* of salvation established by Christ, only in the sacramental system does it appear that grace comes down to us in a visible manner.

Scholastic theology distinguishes between sacramental grace and extrasacramental grace, the latter meaning grace conferred outside the actual reception of the sacraments. Such a distinction is valid only for the theologian who isolates the sacraments from each other and from the Church, and looks upon them as so many separate "mechanisms" destined singly to "cause" a determined measure of grace. We cannot help thinking that such a view of the sacraments is a rather materialistic one, reflecting the atomism that came to the fore in a later theology. It is not far removed from magic—not, of course, "black magic," which is practiced against the will of God, but "white magic," which attempts to dispose of the divine power by means of appropriate formulas. To our way of thinking, the Christians of the Reform and the Oriental Christians are right in protesting against a conception which is influenced by Nominalism, the bane of theology in the fifteenth century, and which unfortunately has infiltrated most theological textbooks and catechisms in the course of the last three centuries.

Sacraments are not vending machines, infusing a certain degree of grace the moment sacramental formulas have been correctly pronounced. Whatever one may say or think, this is a near approach to magic, the negation of all religion. Fortunately, the sacramental practice among fervent Christians is of a better quality than the teaching they have received.

The instant a Christian, animated by faith, allows the

desire to receive a sacrament to well up within him, he puts himself under the influence of the grace proper to that sacrament. This is the teaching of classical theology on the subject of spiritual communion and the act of perfect contrition coupled with the intention of going to confession. We do nothing more here than simply generalize this accredited doctrine and apply it to all the sacraments.

The desire to receive a sacrament could very well be concealed in the sincere will to encounter God, even where few or no authentic sacraments are in acknowledged use, as is the case among the Protestants or indeed among pagans. We apply here the doctrine which says that anyone outside the Church can have a genuine, though possibly inexplicit, desire for the Church, a desire that goes by the name of *votum Ecclesiae*. We are not authorized to separate the sacraments from the Church, for they are the visible and actual sanctifying rites of the Church. But we know that, thanks to the incarnation and the redemption, the whole world has already been sanctified fundamentally. This is the reason that all human symbols, and thus all religious rites, possess a sanctifying value insofar as they do not stand in opposition to the true religion. What they do not possess is the full guarantee of Christ's living presence. They preserve a real ambiguity outside the Church, and on that score can serve to draw men away from God. In this light, all grace seems to us to be sacramental, because all grace implies to some extent the visibility of the Church.

And thus we reach the true nature of the Christian sacraments, that by which they differ in their inner being from all other religious rites and ceremonies.

The main theme of our last sections has been the living presence of the Blessed Trinity. Grace is unthinkable except as the fruit of the indwelling, a subject we shall return to in our next section. The Church, too, is determined in her inner being by that divine and consequently active presence. For indeed, neither the incarnation nor the redemption, the two fundamental mysteries of our faith, are to be thought of apart from the active election by the Father and the Son's mission in obedience and love, in and through the power of the Holy Ghost. We fail to see on what grounds the sacraments would be exceptions. In the sacraments, the fruits of the redemption are applied to us. In them, we are granted grace within the sphere of the Church. In essence, they are modeled on the incarnation. They are in effect symbolic actions (not separate things or separate causes) which, in their visibility, express the invisible divinity. They thereby make the divine present.

Early theologians did not look at the sacraments differently from us. We remember how, during the war years, our dogma professor who taught us the treatise on the sacraments laboriously set out to prove, against the liberal theology of Adolf von Harnack and others, that the early Fathers of the Church understood the sacraments to be "causes of grace." We have nothing against the Western classical theology of the sacraments, provided it is not forgotten that no council has defined this doctrine to be of faith, and that even in the West the "causality" of the sacraments is differently explained by different theologians. Each school has its own theoretical technical elaboration which is not part of the dogma itself.

In any event, the painstaking efforts of our professor failed to satisfy us. Deliverance came to us the day we opened a textbook of Greek Orthodox theology entitled *Dogmatic Theology of the Eastern Orthodox Church*, published in Athens at the beginning of the century. In the chapter called *"Mysteria"* ("The Sacraments"), many texts were quoted from the Fathers of the Church attributing the operation of the sacraments to *the action of the Holy Ghost*. With that, light dawned on us. And indeed, not only was this the teaching of the Fathers; it was the common conception embodied in the liturgy, especially in the Eastern liturgy. The latter, in the administration of the sacraments, contained the prayer *Epiclesis*, specially addressed to the Holy Ghost, invoking Him to fill the water, the chrism and the sacred actions with His power and grace. Nothing more was needed to prove that the older theology had never detached the sacraments from their deeper roots, that it had never considered them apart from the creative, effectual presence of the Father in the Son through the power of the Holy Ghost.

This liberating discovery enabled us to combine our doctrine of the sacraments more definitely and more intimately with the doctrine of grace. Until then, the commonly taught sacramental theology had prevented us from seeing these two matters in their true light. But now we were satisfied that the *one source, the one cause and root of grace is the living presence in us of the Blessed Trinity*. If the sacraments, "confer upon us the grace they signify," as the catechism teaches, then the only source of that grace is none other than the same presence of the Blessed Trinity. And of this the priest is the ordained, visible minister, the representative of the Church or, more in depth, of Christ and His spirit.

God's indwelling is made to bear fruit in us in a visible, experiential manner; at the same time it gathers us all together in order to form us into one people of God, both visible and invisible, the Body of Christ, the Church. By this action, the Father prolongs the work of the redemption in Christ and in the power of His Spirit.

All the sacraments bear out this concept, especially the celebration of the holy eucharist. In the mass the Church is being built up anew, gathered to the Father, and thus sanctified by the Father in the Son through the Holy Ghost.

The Church as Bride

The Church is not only the Body of Christ; she is also His Bride. We regard the Church as the God-given sphere within which we can approach God, return to Him in faith, hope and charity and adore Him in spirit. Here we find again the second movement started in us by the indwelling of the Blessed Trinity, the movement which leads us back to the Father by the power of the Holy Ghost.

This upward movement is not confined to the purely spiritual level. We have to return to God as we are, as men, with souls and bodies, with hearts and hands. In other words, our adoration in spirit must necessarily proceed from us by way of visible acts of religion and worship, as acts of the liturgy established by the Church.

The Christian cult ought to express itself first and foremost in the liturgy of the sacraments. The sacraments have been regarded so exclusively as "efficacious instruments of grace" that people seem to have forgotten that the sacraments are above all prayers and the Church's public acts of worship. Unless we are blind, this should be the very first thing noticed in the sacraments. The wrong understanding of *opus operatum* (the efficacy proper to the sacraments), together with the fact that in the Western Church the sacraments have been administered for centuries in a foreign and practically unknown idiom, has had disastrous consequences. How many of the ordinary faithful are still able to recognize

a prayer-deed in the Latin formulas all too frequently mut-
tered in an unbecoming rush? Someone might glibly answer that the sacraments are efficacious by themselves, and
that the personal holiness and piety of the priest do not
affect their fruitfulness. Things have come to such a pass
that if any priest or layman dares to insist that those fine
sacramental prayers should in all fairness be recited as authentic prayers, that is, with a spirit of adoration, all he
does is arouse surprise. "Another of those fanatics! Another
of those rabid liturgists!" Remarks of this sort have been
heard within the aula of the second Vatican Council.

However unfamiliar and unsuspected it may seem to some,
the sacraments are prayers addressed to God and therefore
public ecclesiastical acts of worship. In these prayers, so
teaches the venerable tradition of Scholasticism, the Church
"expresses her faith" as the Bride of Christ. All those who
participate—he who receives the sacrament, the community
around him and not least the officiating priest, the "steward
of the mysteries of God"—have their appointed task.
Each one takes part in the congregational act of the cult.

We apologize for dwelling at such length on these questions; but to tell the truth, we all need to reform our approach. Matters will improve when the vernacular is reintro-
duced, for it will then be plain to us all how much our
habitual manner of acting is at variance with the words
we utter or hear. Is it not a shame that a more becoming
celebration of the liturgy is found in countries where Catholics are in the minority compared with the Reform Christians, and, as if that were not enough, have entered into
dialogue with the non-Catholics? In so-called Catholic countries or in ghettos, speed and unsuitable muttering are still the
rule. The most striking thing we have come across in our
reading in this domain is an article in an American review,
written before the Council and dealing with the use of the
vernacular in the liturgy. Arguing against the use of the vernacular, the author of the article suggests that the faithful
might be disedified because they could no longer understand why priests are in such a hurry! Is this not topsy-
turvy reasoning? Our Lord has said, "When you pray, do
not go on gabbling like the heathens who fancy that the
more they say, the more likely they are to be heard. You
are not to be like them" (Mt. 6:7-8). We smile at the prayer
drums in use among the lamas of Tibet, and at the hysterical

voodoo rites in the West Indies. But are our "Catholic" liturgical performances any better?

We shall say no more on this subject.

In the acts of Catholic worship, we meet again with grace, which Karl Rahner calls "grace received"; grace existentially accepted and lived up to, grace that comes to life in faith and charity. This aspect of grace is as trinitarian as the former ones.

On a previous page, we have seen how, according to St. Paul, we are not able to pray the Our Father except in the Holy Ghost (Rom. 8:15-16; Gal. 4:3). "I tell you . . . no one can say: Jesus is the Lord [the earliest Christian profession of faith] unless it be in the Holy Ghost" (I Cor. 12:3). "In the same way the Spirit comes to the aid of our weakness. When we do not know how to pray, the Spirit himself pleads for us through our inarticulate groans. And he who can read hearts [an Old Testament description of God the Father] knows well what the Spirit means: he intercedes for the saints according to the mind of God" (Rom. 8:26-27). No one ever stated more plainly that in prayer, and thus also in grace, God does not exactly come down to our level; instead, He grants us a share in the inner life of the Trinity—a share shrouded on earth in the obscurity of the faith.

Our prayer, then, is carried up by the Holy Ghost; we must add that it does not reach the Father except "through our Lord Jesus Christ," as the liturgy says in the final words of its orations. We would look in vain for a better comprehensive view of Christian prayer than the closing words of the canon of the mass. A moment or two before intoning the Pater, the priest takes in hand both the consecrated bread and the chalice, lifts them in one gesture toward the Father and says, "through Him, and with Him, and in Him, be to You, God and Father, in union with the Holy Ghost, all honor and glory."

This prayer shows plainly that the celebration of the eucharist, so central as the sanctifying source of grace and union with God, is no less central as the act of adoration of the Christian cult; it is performed by Christian society as a whole, gathered round the High Priest Jesus Christ.

Incidentally, to correct a false notion, we will observe here that Catholics do not go to mass on Sundays only because the Church obliges them to do so under pain of mortal sin. To be prompted to action merely by the threat of mortal sin is to fall into rank legalism. It should be well understood that we go to Sunday mass because the eucharistic sacrifice is for us Catholics the highest form of that public and private adoration which we owe to the Father in the Son through the Holy Ghost. The faithful who neglect to do so fall grievously short of their duty to sanctify the Lord's day with the noblest act of worship instituted for the purpose by Christ Himself.

This is the reason the Church has had to warn us that the knowing and willful omission of Sunday mass is of its nature, not in virtue of an additional law, a grave offense against the divine majesty—so grave, in fact, that it cannot be less than a mortal sin. An adequate understanding of this point requires that we rid ourselves of an individualistic outlook on life. Religion is not a private affair, engaging only the individual and his conscience. For in our capacity as members of the people of God gathered round the altar on Sundays, we are subject to serious community obligations. Only he who has grasped the truth that the life of grace and personal piety are inseparable from the Church, from our visible and invisible association in Christ, is in a position to appreciate the full beauty of the mass and its profound significance for man's life.

By now, the reader will agree that the numerous aspects of the faith not only complement each other but basically form one single, simple reality. To convince ourselves of this, we have merely to view them in the pure light of faith rather than consider them as a bewildering maze of laws and impositions, a collection of points of faith and religious opinions that have nothing in common except the fortuitous character of being accepted in the lump by Roman Catholics.

Conclusion

We have come to the end of this important chapter. We began by listening at some length to Holy Scripture, which in varying tones and themes extols our intimate association in Christ. We learned of our condition as God's visible people on earth, the new Israel, which is the external manifestation of what binds us together in depth, like brothers and sisters in Christ. We have shown how this state springs from the Father's election and is brought about by the moving power of the Holy Ghost. We then considered the point more closely and analyzed it in systematic detail—how in the Church we share in the "living life" of the Blessed Trinity that comes to us from the Father in the Son through the Holy Ghost, and how, in virtue of the divine "philanthropy," we are led back to the Father in Christ through the consummating love of the Spirit.

Created and Uncreated Grace

Let us first of all define the two rather unfamiliar notions of created and uncreated grace. A bird's-eye view of the historical growth of the first notion will permit us to reduce the reality it signifies to its proper limits. We shall take pains to show that created grace has no existence as a distinct actuality, but that by its inner dynamism it connects us with the Trinity. Each time in the past theologians overlooked this significant aspect, they provoked objections which sometimes had tragic consequences, as for instance in the days of the Reformation when whole sections of Christendom fell away from the Church. I do not maintain that the atrophy of the notion of created grace was the only cause of the Reformation, but it supplied a motive for protest against the then current Catholic theology; it does so still now.

Origin of These Notions

In theology, *uncreated grace* stands for God Himself insofar as He communicates Himself to man in love. In contradistinction to this, *created grace* signifies the result God's Self-communication produces on man. Evidently that result cannot be God Himself; therefore, it is something other than God, something created, a gift from God.

The notion of created grace has remained practically unknown in the East, and in the West it took eleven centuries to become a clearly defined and conscious concept. In Scripture the word *grace* represented a rather fluid idea. Where no further precision was added, it referred above all to the love which is God Himself, or to the presence of that love in us. Thus it implied the eventual grace which God worked out in us in consequence of His presence.

A time came when something more definite was needed in order to answer several questions raised about basic points of faith. A first question was: if the baptism of children has any real meaning—as defined by several councils in past centuries—what exactly do the children receive, considering that they are still incapable of evincing personal acts of faith and charity? Scripture seemed to indicate clearly enough that no one is sanctified and justified without acts of faith and charity; how then could children be sanctified by baptism? Then came a second question, akin to the first. After we have been sanctified by divine grace, we *remain* children of God; we live in a "state of grace." Yet it is evident that we do not uninterruptedly make acts of faith and charity. What then do we mean when we say that we have received the "virtue" of charity, or that we live in a "state of grace"?

These are simple queries; some might call them naive. But they betray a real need. The same questions are still being asked today. Dealing with the problem became a custom in professional theology even after Peter Lombard, toward the middle of the twelfth century, risked a rather daring reply to the second question. In his celebrated work *Sententiarum libri quattuor,* he quoted Paul's words: "For the love of God has been poured into our hearts by the Holy Ghost who has been given us" (Rom. 5:15). From this text he drew the hardy conclusion: our love is precisely the Holy Ghost Who has been given to us. Lombard's work served as a textbook in all the monasteries and universities of Europe till well into the sixteenth century. Every prospective teacher of theology had to start upon his academic career with a series of lectures commenting on the *Sententiae.* Every professor of theology had to face that conclusion of Lombard's and undertake the delicate task of giving it an acceptable meaning. And thus the problem of how the Holy Ghost, as uncreated gift, is related to charity, as created gift in us, came to the fore in terms at once pregnant and insistent. To accept Lombard's bold paradox literally was tantamount to denying all personal activity in the practice of Christian charity. But the respect paid to the *Magister*

Sententiarum, as Lombard was called, and the respect due to Scripture made it impossible for theologians simply to bypass the problem raised in those terms.

St. Thomas solved the question in a masterly way, though from too narrow a point of view. This present book is not the place to enter into St. Thomas' technical theological formulas; the reader will be presumed to have some familiarity with the philosophy and theology of Aquinas' time. In the proposed explanation that follows, we shall remain true to St. Thomas' fundamental intuition. It will be more profitable, however, to bring to light the permanent elements which entered into the conflicting opinions of the successive schools and which are still instructive today. History, they say, teaches us how to live; it also teaches us how to think. Faulty thinking processes should be carefully avoided, for they never fail to stir up the same reactions. The point we are dealing with is ample proof of this. The question facing us now is: what is the relation between God as gift and His grace conferred on us? Or, how do created and uncreated grace stand in relation to each other?

Luther's Doctrine

The young Luther, while still a Catholic monk, wrote against the doctrine of grace current in his day. But he himself had been brought up in this theology; he knew no other, though he was familiar with the German mystics and, of course, with St. Augustine, for he belonged to the order of the Augustinians. And soon, as a youthful professor at Wittenberg, he would be applying himself wholeheartedly to the study of the Bible. The theology of his time would be of no use to him in the pursuit of biblical studies; it could at best irritate him—to some extent, rightly.

What had happened in the theological world meanwhile? Ever since created grace had been cut off from its one and only source, that is, from the interior operation of the indwelling Holy Ghost, it had come to look increasingly like a personal possession, some sort of capital that could be treasured up or put to use at will. From this, an impression could be gained that man acquired some rights before God merely by making good use of that capital. Professional theologians would have been careful not to draw such a conclusion; but the common preacher, who often made short work of prudent nuances in theology, had come to a rather crude notion of what grace is. This, together with the miserable traffic in indulgences at the time and the corruption in ecclesiastical life, was sufficient ground for protest, even for justifiable protest.

We are of the opinion that Luther's initial protest was in fact justified. In his Catholic days, his theology was not always safe: nor was that of many Catholics of the period. It is quite impossible, of course, to form an idea of what Luther's personal conscience was in the later stages of his evolution. Today, no one denies that the Church needed reform. The deep emotion stirred up within him by what he had witnessed in the Church, and perhaps also (as Karl Meissinger, a well-known Protestant historian, surmises) the enormous success he met with in whole regions of Europe, drove him to excess, to a radicalism that ended with expulsion from the Church. We are at one with Professor W. H. van de Pol in thinking that the poor man, distraught with warring doubts, finally could no longer accept the belief that the visible Church he saw around him was still the Church of Christ. If what we wrote in a previous section has any value, then we can see that it is impossible to reform the Church from outside; reform must come from within. That was Luther's misfortune.

What was Luther's teaching concerning grace? Scripture is explicit enough: we are justified *only* through grace; and we can assert no right whatever to it. Created grace is consequently unable to bind God to us. William of Ockham had already said as much. Luther carried Ockham's reaction to an impassioned rebellion and thus fell to the other extreme: it is meaningless to speak of *created* grace in any sense, or of any *interior* justifications; we are justified *sola gratia,* that is, *exclusively* through grace. And saying this, he stood by the principal meaning attached to grace in Scripture, namely, God's love for us. Nothing further! He solved the problem of the relationship between created grace and uncreated grace by eliminating one of the terms of the problem.

However, he was too close as yet to Catholic tradition to be satisfied with such a doctrinal simplification. So he kept other elements of the Catholic faith, twisting them into an extreme form of radicalism because of his strong aversion to the ideas commonly received in the schools. As we understand matters, Luther at bottom did nothing else than reject the visible Church he knew in his Catholic days. And therefore, among other things, the one principle of authority he admitted for his religious beliefs was *sola Scriptura*, that is, God speaking to us *exclusively* in Scripture. In this light, the words *sola fide*—by faith alone—which he discovered in the Epistle to the Romans acquire a unique significance. Man is justified neither by his works, nor by any kind of merit, but *exclusively* by faith. Justification is not something granted to him, but "imputed" to him, insofar as God covers his sins with the merits of Christ. And that is why man is justified—only because of Christ. Christ's merits are the sole ground of man's trust in God. Our justification rests on Christ alone and not on ourselves.

Let us add that Luther, and after him more explicitly Calvin, did not at all deny the operation of the Holy Ghost moving us to lead Christian lives. Most Catholic textbooks dealing with the subject take no notice whatever of this point. In Luther's view, we are really sanctified already in this life. This sanctification, however, is of no value *coram Deo* (in the sight of God), that is, here on earth, where only an absolute obedience to the divine sanctity and majesty could be of *any worth*. Here on earth we remain imperfect. Nothing imperfect can enter God's presence. And in this fundamental respect, halfway obedience is already formal disobedience. In the presence of God's absolute sanctity, there can be no talk of greater or smaller sins.

Therefore, God cannot but condemn us as sinners. At the same time, however, He deigns out of sheer mercy to cover with the merits of Christ this sin of ours, so deep-set in our nature. That is why we are simultaneously sinners and just men. We shall not understand this basic Protestant paradox unless we take into account that Luther, and after him the Reformation as a whole, was the offspring and heir of Nominalism. Nominalism drove a wedge into reality and wrenched it asunder by distinguishing in it two orders of reality: the absolute order of God's freedom and the order of God's providence chosen once and for all. That is how the Reformation, and above all Lutheranism, drew a distinction within our human actuality between the Kingdom of God and the kingdom of men, that is, the state; between the sphere of our interior sanctification and the absolute extent of our justification.

Whatever Luther preserved of the divine indwelling,

known to him through the traditional teaching of mysticism, comes into the open only in the order of our sanctification; and this he now and then qualified as *coram hominibus*, that is, in our dealings with other men. Within the latter sphere, which is the sphere of the Church, we may reach a certain degree of Christian perfection. But *coram Deo*, in the sight of God, the indwelling is nothing more than God's love which, in sheer mercy, sets us free because of Christ's merits. Without justifying us interiorly, the divine love considers us as just men already, exclusively for Christ's sake. In his own way, Luther rediscovered the personal relations existing between God and man which the barren Scholastic speculations had lost sight of. This would account for the success of his teaching, despite its departures from orthodoxy.

The Answer of Trent

If the Church intended to take into account this "reformed adjustment," she had to show how all human relations with God, without exception, can be reduced to *one living contact*, the contact we have in the indwelling of the Blessed Trinity. It was the tragedy of the times that such an attempt could not be made then because the theology of those days was powerless to elaborate a truly satisfying answer. Several centuries later, Cardinal Newman would guess the ecumenical significance of an adequate answer when he wrote the Catholic foreword to the new edition of his formerly Anglican *Lectures on Justification*; but by that time it was too late. Christendom lay riven apart for ages.

What was the answer the Church of the sixteenth century eventually brought to the question? It was the answer formulated by the Council of Trent. Since the Middle Ages, the popes had given their approval to the development of theological thought, especially in regard to the data of faith connected with the baptism of children. The Council of Vienne (France) in 1312 declared that "the teaching which says that in baptism of both children and adults, informing grace and virtues are given, is more probable and in better harmony and agreement with what the saints and the modern doctors of theology have said" (Denz. 483). When we spoke of Ockham, we pointed out that this doctrine was commonly accepted in the Church toward the end of the Middle Ages.

The Council of Trent thus had to answer the objections of the Reformers who rejected this ecclesiastical teaching. That answer, of course, was not easy to give. To begin with, most theologians and bishops present at the Council had been trained along Nominalistic lines and were possessed of no better theology than that which Luther had received in his early religious formation. Further, as all the preceding councils had done, Trent intended to hold to the principle of not settling questions freely debated among Catholics. Trent quite intentionally confined itself to condemning Luther's positions insofar as these had drifted away from the Church's general teaching. The clearest formula rebutting the Lutheran position is to be found in the following text taken from Chapter 7 of the *Decree on Justification*: "Finally, the one formal cause [of our justification] is the justice of God, not the one by which He Himself is just, but the one with which He makes us just [this is a quotation from St. Augustine]. And this means that by this gift of His we are renewed in our spirit, and that we are not merely reputed to be so [that is, justice is not merely imputed to us], but that we are really called just and indeed are just, by the fact that each one of us receives his own justice in the measure the Holy Ghost destines to each one (I Cor. 12:11) and according to each one's disposition and cooperation" (Denz. 799).

All that Trent could do was reaffirm the general truth in Holy Writ which had been specially and rather precisely formulated in the Western Church in the doctrine of created grace—that through created grace we have become truly just and holy. Trent, however, did not want to use the term *created grace,* and satisfied itself with less technical phrasing which kept closer to Scripture and steered clear of the controversies within the Church. Thus, the Council said that justice "inheres in us," *nobis inhaeret.*

In point of fact, Trent does not seem to have noticed the question at issue: what is the relation between uncreated and created grace? The theology of those days could not tackle the problem. And in that sense it may be said that Trent did not provide a complete answer to the deeper religious objections raised by the Reformation. In fairness, though, it should be admitted that Trent did say something on the subject. Several Lutherans have acknowledged to us that in the last conciliar chapter, dealing with merit, suggestions were made but not fully worked out. That section, which happens to be the most religious one in the *Decree on Justification,* is Chapter 16: "The Fruits of Justification, That Is, the Merit of Good Works and the Nature of That Merit." It is worth noticing that Trent did not take an easy way out of the problem; it looked at it from all angles in a sort of dialectical movement, starting from God and returning to God. We quote at length:

Therefore, to men justified in this manner, whether they have preserved uninterruptedly the grace received or have recovered it when lost, the words of the Apostle have to be pointed out: "Abound in every good work, knowing that your labor is not in vain in the Lord" (I Cor. 15:58); "for God is not unjust that he should forget your work and the love which you have shown in his name" (Heb. 6:10); and "do not lose your confidence, which has a great reward" (Heb. 10:35). And so, to those who work well to the end (Mt. 10:22) and trust in God, *eternal life is to be offered, both as a grace mercifully promised to the sons of God through Christ Jesus* and as a reward promised by God Himself, to be faithfully given to their good works and merits. For this is the "crown of justice" which the Apostle declared was laid up for him after his fight and course to be rendered by the just judge, and not only to him but also to all who love His coming (II Tim. 4:7-8). *For since Christ Jesus Himself, as the head of His members* (Eph. 4:15) *and as the vine of which we are the branches* (Jn. 15:5), *continuously infuses strength into those justified, a strength which always precedes, accompanies and follows their good works and without which they could not in any way be pleasing and meritorious before God,* we must believe that nothing further is wanting to those justified to prevent them from being considered, by those very works which have been done in God, to have fully satisfied the divine law according to the state of this life and to have truly merited eternal life. And this eternal life is to be obtained in [its] due time, provided they die in grace; for Christ our Savior says, "If anyone shall drink of the water that I will give him, he shall not thirst forever; but it shall become in him a fountain of water springing up unto life everlasting" (Jn. 4:14). Thus, neither is our justice established as our own from ourselves, nor is the justice of God ignored or repudiated; for the justice which we call ours because we are justified by its inhering in us, *that same justice is from God, because it is infused into us by God through the merits of Christ.*

Nor should this be omitted, that Christ promises the person who even gives a drink of cold water to one of His least ones that he shall not be without reward (Mt. 10:42), and the Apostle says that our present light affliction, which is for the moment, prepares for us an eternal weight of glory that is beyond all measure (II Cor. 4:17). Although in Holy Scripture much high value is placed on good works, nevertheless, *no Christian should either trust or glory in himself and not in the Lord* (I Cor. 1:31; II Cor. 10:17), Whose goodness toward all men is such that He wants His gifts to be their merits.

And since we all offend in many things (Jas. 3:2), each one should have before his eyes not only God's mercy and goodness but also His justice and severity. Neither should anyone pass judgment on his own life, even if he is conscious of no wrong; for the whole of man's life is to be examined and judged not by the judgment of men but of God, He "who will bring to light the hidden things of darkness, and will make manifest the counsels of hearts; and then every man shall have his praise from God" (I Cor. 4:5) Who, as it is written, will render to everyone according to his works (Rom. 2:6; Ps. 62:13). [Denz. 809-810]

We have printed in italics the conciliar statements which affirm that our good works can be of value in the eyes of God only insofar as they have been done *in loving union with Christ*. Post-Tridentine theologians should have considered it their task to develop this idea to the fullest. Unfortunately, they did not; it was rather the other way around. After Trent, Catholic theology continued to shut itself into an ever more rigid and defensive position. During the following three or four centuries, theologians satisfied themselves mainly with substantiating the existence of created grace. By and large, they failed to give serious thought to what is in fact the ultimate root of man's interior sanctification: the living indwelling of the Blessed Trinity. And so created grace was understood by the ordinary faithful to be a thing by itself. Only one connection with God was still kept in mind, namely, that it is a gift from God, and is therefore something created. At this juncture, there remained but one more step to be taken, a step, alas, all too often ventured upon in sermons and popular writings: grace, when conferred on man, became his own possession, so to say, a sort of capital that could be stored up and made to yield abundant returns for heaven. Whenever such notions take root in the mind, the doctrine of grace turns into a caricature of what Holy Scripture and the grand tradition of the Church have always taught.

Atrophy and Reaction

Theologians, steering clear of the Reformers' objections, attached to the sacramental character a meaning it never had. What they took away from grace—likeness and union with Christ—they henceforth attributed to the character. Unfortunately, here as elsewhere, the serious danger arose of conceiving this likeness as a static entity. Spirituality sought for a solution in a more personal love for Christ. But loose from its theological moorings, loose from a solid theology of grace, such a spirituality was threatened with various forms of sentimentalism that really had nothing in common with genuine piety. Sacramental teaching came perilously close to magic—the belief that, by uttering certain formulas, one can automatically procure a determined quantity of divine power. Instead of answering the objections raised by the Reformers, this theology prepared for our "separated brethren" still further grounds for scandal. Happily, the life of faith lived personally by many Catholics was of a better quality than the doctrine served out to them either in religious instructions or from the pulpit.

Many factors ministered to the hardening of this theological position. In the first place, historically, the bitter wars of religion arose in large areas of Europe; one of their results was that human contacts between Protestants and Catholics became practically impossible. In the second place, one form of Catholic theology still paid attention to the Reformation, and that was controversial theology; but controversy has always proved to be a barren variety of theological thinking. In the line of pastoral theology too, the one concern was for self-defense. Further still, when there followed in the wake of the Reformation the *Aufklärung,* then rationalism, the French Revolution and liberalism, and much later Marxism, the Roman Church seemed to build itself into a religious fortress whose defensive walls rose higher and higher. Is it not typical of such a religious attitude that Cardinal Ottaviani gathered together his various addresses and articles about the Church of our days under the significant title *Il Baluardo,* the bulwark, and thus a ghetto, closed up in itself?

The theology of grace had to bear the consequences of all this. The doctrine of grace, as set forth in classrooms and textbooks, was reduced to an uninviting short chapter on what had come to be called "sanctifying grace" and long chapters dealing with the endless disputes on the subject of "actual grace." The divine indwelling, no longer the indwelling of the Blessed Trinity, was lost sight of as the living ground and source of created grace. Instead, it was turned into an immediate consequence, a necessary fruit of infused grace—an extremely impoverished understanding, indeed, of what Scripture teaches.

The mind asks itself in amazement how such a theological position came about. Two causes can be singled out. To begin with, one of the principles belonging to the treatise on the Trinity was being wrongly applied. It was held that the Godhead in its unity of nature was alone involved in the creative act, and not the three divine Persons in Their distinctive properties. It seems to me that this principle deserves to be applied with more nuance than is usually the case in our present-day manuals of theology. St. Thomas was certainly aware of this, though we cannot enter into that question right now. Where grace was concerned, the way of reasoning used to be quite plain: if grace is to be conceived as something exclusively *created,* it comes to us from God in His unity of nature, whence it follows that it unites us to the Godhead and not to the Trinity. The indwelling can at best be "attributed" to the Holy Ghost, in a derived sense only. And this was done for the sake of putting things in the traditional way and speaking like Scripture. Here is a clear instance of what may be expected when theological thought fails to listen attentively to what the word of God has to say in Holy Writ.

A second cause for the decline of the treatise on grace has been a too-wooden interpretation of the first text we quoted from the Tridentine decree. The text says that the infused justice, which is in us and "inheres in us," is also the "one formal cause" of our justification. That being so, theologians thought, it follows that the Catholic doctrine of grace must be based exclusively on "created grace." Such a faulty interpretation is, of course, foreign to the mind of the Fathers of Trent and consequently devoid of all value: it has no authority to bind us in faith.

In short, many theologians were persuaded that the more the Protestants attacked created grace, the more they themselves had to fix their attention on created grace. Let us say in passing, however, that a small minority among the theologians kept protesting through the centuries against the latter assumption. These were never very numerous, but their contribution was of a high quality. They deliberately based themselves on the teaching of Scripture or on the doctrine of the ancient Fathers and the mystical tradition of the Middle Ages. Among our own countrymen of the sixteenth century, we may point out Leonard Lessius and Cornelius a Lapide. Lessius was deeply influenced by Ruysbroeck, whom he sought to defend against detractors; and A Lapide was an outstanding Scripture scholar. During the seventeenth century, we meet two great patrologists, Denys Petau and Christian Thomasius. During the nineteenth century, we have the theologian M. J. Scheeben and the patrologist Théodore de Régnon. At the turn of this century, G. J. Waffelaert, Bishop of Bruges (Belgium), rediscovered Ruysbroeck, and by his writings initiated a renewal of mystical theology in the Netherlands. These theologians were few and far between, and were as a rule considered unsafe by the professionals of their day. As it happened, their authority and their evidence prevented the doctrine of grace from straying into a blind alley.

Finally, Father Maurice de la Taille and after him Father Karl Rahner contributed a wider view of the technical theological explanation which St. Thomas had provided in his time, adding to its persuasive force. Conditions in theology were such that theologians could still be convinced by Scholastic proofs, which explains why De la Taille and Rahner stood a better chance of succeeding than their predecessors had. Within a very short time, De la Taille's key solution made its mark in Europe, and it was soon after still better received in English-speaking countries, especially in America, where a theology thought out in Scholastic concepts is still preferred. Many theologians in Europe, while appreciating De la Taille's theory in spite of its limitations, felt that his basic intuition could be improved upon by being expressed in personalistic categories of thought. Two world wars, a completely new start in biblical studies and in the teaching of the Fathers and the mystics, modern philosophy and ecumenism have set theologians free from too cramping an association with Scholasticism.

Whatever the method employed, the battle is won. We are at long last fit to face resolutely the question which every theologian prior to the Council of Trent was confronted with —to answer the extreme paradox set down by Lombard. However, it is no longer Lombard who compels us to reflect on the problem; it is Scripture itself, together with the teaching of the early Fathers and theologians, the glorious mystical tradition of the Middle Ages and, last but not least, direct dialogues with our "separated brethren" of both the Reform and the Eastern Churches.

The question before us is: what exactly is the relationship between uncreated grace, that is, God Himself or the Blessed Trinity, and our created grace? We can now give an answer.

The Answer to Lombard's Paradox

In the historical survey we gave above, we purposely stayed away from technical theological discussions that suppose some familiarity with the hypotheses of Scholastic theology. At the same time we did not attempt to introduce nuances that could have delineated more sharply the main outlines of the theological evolution. That long and often sad history—does it not concern the glory of the Gospel message?—is more complex than could be shown in the short space of a few lines. We hope that our brief survey has not been too obscure for the uninitiated or too elementary for those conversant with the subject matter.

Priests and laity should know enough of the history of theological thought to appreciate the motives underlying contemporary reactions. The gratitude many of them expressed after reading the first edition of this work indicates that the time has come to write a new treatise on grace for the use of the laity. We may therefore dispense with all manner and forms of concepts which view created grace in terms of abstract geometry.

History bears out the contention that the notion of created grace is not entitled to the central place which it has usurped in the treatise of grace. Prior to the eleventh century, generations of orthodox theologians thought and wrote without ever so much as mentioning created grace. We do not insinuate that recent developments in the consciousness of the Church have to be repudiated. The course of history is irreversible. Furthermore, this development has been approved in some of its salient results by popes and councils, albeit discreetly. Undeniably, "created grace" has meaning, though it is *not* an independent entity, and still less something that becomes our possession, that we can dispose of at will or glory in before God as the fruit of our own strength and endeavor. Created grace, seen in its inner nature, belongs to a higher unity. It is to be thought of only *within* and *not next to* or *apart from* the mystery of the trinitarian indwelling in us. This demands some explanation.

The Grace of the Encounter

Let us begin with an illustration. When a seal is stamped on soft sealing wax, this sticky mass receives the impression of whatever is marked on the metal stamp, like arms or a motto. In that operation, activity proceeds from the pressure exercised by the seal on the wax. The seal itself, however, remains unaltered. The wax is formed in the image of the seal.

Our comparison has one disadvantage. Sealing wax is totally passive. But man is not. Under the divine influx, man not only remains completely free but is granted a new and higher freedom. And this being so, it would be wise to avoid, as much as possible, using illustrations from the material order. Our inborn tendency to depersonalize grace, and whatever belongs to the order of grace, is already strong enough. If grace is love, it is freedom as well; it is given to free men in order to intensify their freedom still more. Our perspective is wrong if we do not keep this in sight.

But let us hark back to the parable of the young man in love with a straying girl. Until the young man met her, the girl remained lonely, destitute and embittered. He did not start by changing her within in order to meet her afterwards. This supposition would make no sense. But then, why say so when speaking of God's dealings with man? Has He first to create grace in us and then, as the fruit of grace, to come and dwell in us?

It was only while the encounter was in progress that the girl really began to be transformed inside. Of this transformation their being together was but the sign and the preparation. Their bodily presence continued to play an active role later. Men cannot draw close to each other in love without a minimum of visible, tangible contact. The young man's love expressed itself spontaneously in his attitude, in his gestures and gifts. He tried regularly to meet the girl. In a previous section we showed that God respects this law of our nature which He has created. The Blessed Trinity came in search of us in Christ, the visibility of the Father in the Holy Ghost. The divine presence stays with us in the Church, the Body of Christ.

Togetherness or bodily presence becomes meaningful whenever it occurs in love. The young man surrendered himself and all he had. He began to speak of himself, of his own life, his home, his joys and worries, his dreams and ideals; he spoke of what he discovered in her, of what they could achieve together. He gave her whatever he bore in himself—his inner peace, his rich interior life and his happiness. The small presents he left her had value only because they came from him and reminded her of him; they were something of him, or they were something they had admired together, something he prized himself. A woman can be bought with money and costly presents, but her heart is to be won with delicate attentions and with beauty, with what one sets great store by.

Just because the young man gave her whatever he had, beginning with what was highest and dearest to him, the girl began to change within. It was the gift of himself, his self-surrendering love, which cured her, raised her to his own level and introduced her into his world. May we not say that we have here two actual effects of grace: the effect of healing us; and the effect of introducing us into the intimacy of God, of making us share already on earth in the life of the Son with the Father in the power of the Holy Ghost?

The one flaw in our parable lies in the fact that no man can boast of being powerful enough to add anything to the personal worth of another. Man is imperfect; he needs another as much as another needs him. But with God the case is different. His love is a creative love. No sooner is His love directed toward us, no sooner does it come down to us, than we are changed by it within. The moment God loves us, we are forthwith attracted to Him from within. We feel urged toward Him. His love wakens in us a hunger for His presence, a thirst for His life. *And that precisely is created grace.* It takes its rise, grows and lives thanks to His presence. As St. Augustine said, *"Quia amasti me, fecisti me ama-*

bilem," "Because You have loved me, You have made me lovable."

Grace Healing Us

We can express this truth in a more abstract manner for the benefit of those who desire to reflect on their faith in a more rationally conscious way. To do so, we shall proceed along the lines of St. Thomas' fundamental intuition, as further elaborated recently by De la Taille and Rahner.

Basically, the mystery of grace rests on the fact that God gives Himself to us. He grants us an immediate share in His life. He comes down to us, or to speak more accurately, He takes us up into His inner glory. We remain men, creatures and sinners, but as men we are enabled to share in His life because *He gives Himself to us immediately,* that is, without anything intervening between Him and us.

This would be impossible, however, unless man was "adapted" to his new condition. For of ourselves we stand outside this new existence; we have no claim to such a life. We possess neither the strength nor even the aptitude to raise ourselves to such heights, to penetrate unaided into the divine glory.

The interior "adaptation" of our human nature, called in theological terms *dispositio ultima,* has two aspects. God's sanctity condemns sin; He can do nothing else. Consequently, His indwelling love *heals* our sinfulness, not just on the surface, not merely by diminishing the number of our misdeeds, not by "not imputing" our sins, but by attacking the seed of sin, of pride and self-glorification. To that end, His indwelling love sows in us the seed of love.

The healing is an actual gift. We are no longer sinners; we have become in fact children of God. Nevertheless, the healing process remains the task of a lifetime. We are indeed just; and we have to become still more just till the day when we shall be fully so in heaven. God respects our nature. Man needs time to become himself, to grow and to ripen slowly. Hence the words of Trent, in the chapter on merit which was quoted earlier: ". . . we must believe that nothing further is wanting to those justified to prevent them from being considered, by those very works which have been done in God, to have fully satisfied the divine law according to the state of this life. . . ." Luther, in his radical outlook, failed to understand this great mercy of God. At the end of the same chapter, Trent added a last warning: "And since we all offend in many things (Jas. 3:2), each one should have before his eyes not only God's mercy and goodness but also His justice and severity." Sanctifying grace, infused in us by baptism as created grace, is the fundamental orientation of our person, the immersion of our will in the love which we have freely received thanks to the power of the indwelling Spirit, and to which we must give an ever more actualized expression throughout our lives. This is not possible without growth in sanctity. In a former section we characterized the healing aspect of created grace as a share in Christ's obedience. Through grace, we become obedient servants of God in the Servant.

Grace Elevating Us

The other aspect of grace is that the Father, through His indwelling love, introduces us into the very life of the divine Persons. We are chosen to stand before the Father with the Son in the strength of Their mutual Spirit. Through grace, therefore, we become children of God in the Son. In theological language this is called the *elevating* aspect of grace, because of which a truly *super*natural life arises in us. A moment ago we mentioned that we were unable by our own effort to free ourselves from the anathema of sin; now we have to say that it is absolutely unthinkable that we should raise ourselves by our unaided effort to the level of the divine life, which is God's sovereign possession. Our elevation is an utterly gratuitous gift, the totally unexpected surprise the message of grace holds in store for us.

Before we are brought to God's sanctity, our human nature needs to be "adapted": it must be purified of all sin. This is not juridical fiction; it is rather the divine gift of forgiveness. When God forgives, His pardon is an actual fact. His pardon means a deliverance. "Adaptation" is still more radically required in order that we be fit to share in the divine life, which is beyond our powers. Sanctifying grace prepares us for the supernatural participation, fits us for such a life. "For the love of God has been poured into our hearts through the Holy Ghost who has been given us" (Rom. 5:5).

At this moment we again recall the text and commentary of Lombard which caused such headaches to so many of his successors. In our quality of sons in the Son, we are henceforth really capable of loving His Father and our Father, His God and our God, through the invincible power of the Spirit Who has been given to us and Who dwells in us. It is indeed *our* love, our puny, wretched, human love, but love borne aloft from within and perfected by the love of the Spirit. For Trent said, in the chapter we have just cited, "His goodness toward men is so great that He desires His own gifts to be their merits"—yet another of the many texts from St. Augustine adopted by the Council. We should add this: God's love for men is so great that He wants His own love to be our love. And He alone has the power to make it so by causing His love to permeate, perfect and animate our love, and by transforming it to bring it back to Himself.

It should be abundantly clear by now that created grace may not be conceived of apart from the divine indwelling. We have endeavored to show this from history. The nature of grace itself must bear it out and convince us. Created grace is not something standing *in between* God and us; it is no path to approach God, no ladder to climb up to God, no *means* to God—at least, not primarily. But these are negative concepts; unless we go beyond such representations of grace, we shall make no progress in knowledge. The Eastern Christians are quite justified when they refuse to accept such descriptions of grace. They find it self-evident, to put it rather bluntly, that creaturehood plus created grace cannot possibly bring about a divine life or constitute a share in the divine life.

Created grace does not act as a screen between God and us since it comes into being only because of and within the gesture by which God unites us immediately to Himself. He gives Himself without an intervening medium; He comes to dwell in us and takes us back to Himself. Émile Mersch called this grace *"un être d'union,"* "a unifying being." Created grace is at once the fruit and the bond of the indwelling, originating in the indwelling and sustained by the indwelling; it raises us into an ever-deepening actualization of the indwelling on earth and in heaven. Latin expresses it more tersely: *ex unione, in unione et ad unionem*—arising from our immediate union with God, granted in that union and urging us to that union. We need a dynamic concept, one that lives because it is enveloped in "the living life" which is none other than God Himself.

A Personal Relationship

To illustrate still better what we have in mind, we had an occasion to be present in the summer of 1961 at a recital in New York by the well-known singer Joan Sutherland. Thousands of people had flocked to the colossal Lewisohn Stadium. The Stadium is so enormous that nothing more could be seen of the singer than a lustrous green spot on an immense podium in the blaze of the high-powered lights. When people go to a recital, they want not only to hear the singing but to watch its interpretation as a whole—the delivery, the expression, the fire animating the singer. Fortunately, we had brought our opera glasses with us. And these enabled us to establish *personal contact* with the singer in spite of the distance. Why otherwise would we take the trouble of going to a concert when machines at our disposal could reproduce the sound better than it was at the actual performance?

To return to our subject matter, did it matter whether our opera glasses were made of gold or of plastic or of steel, in Japan or in Germany? The one thing of interest to us was Joan Sutherland; and that was reason enough to be glad that we had not forgotten the glasses. We wanted to see in her eyes, in her face, in her gestures whatever it was she intended to convey to us. Any piece of art is a message of beauty. That message comes into its own when it is presented by a living person. So we were grateful for the glasses because they gave us a living contact; they linked us with her.

Much of this is applicable to grace. It is of no great consequence to know how many kinds of grace there are, and what they could be called or how they could be defined and described. The main point is that grace enables us to live in *personal contact* with God. Created grace has no other *raison d'être*.

"Because You have loved me, You have made me lovable!" This suggests another thought, which the renowned apostle of reunion, the Abbé Couturier, was fond of introducing when the conversation happened to touch upon true Christian charity. It is often said that charity is a gift of self. But a subtle brand of pride may lie concealed in this definition. We are conscious that *we* have something to give. Does not the greatest love consist in *allowing others* to love us and to give us something of themselves? This thought gives us the key to the mystery of grace. And it is along those lines that we must recast the saying of St. Augustine: "Because You have loved us, we are now able to love You."

Increase and Decrease of Grace

In the light of the foregoing sections, we grasp clearly how senseless it would be to look upon grace as privately owned capital which we would like to see increase. It is foolish to stand, ruler in hand, on the alert to measure the grace we may have "merited." The increase or decrease of grace is as much dependent on our surrender to God in grace as on any other factor. We cannot sufficiently emphasize the fact that grace is never automatically granted apart from our free surrender through faith and love. This idea allows us to unmask still another wrongheaded notion about grace.

Grace undoubtedly can increase, and we can, according to Trent, merit this increase. But that has nothing to do with quantity; it merely implies a qualitative intensification of grace. All theologians are in agreement on this point. Despite this, one comes across a trend in classical theology, especially marked during recent centuries, which we think has failed to free itself from the dangerous notion of automatism. As we see it, that notion is a perverted one. It could spread only in circles where the concept of "reified" grace has gained ground.

To speak of an increase or decrease in grace makes sense only when we place ourselves on the personal level of a living encounter between God and man. The Council of Trent defined, in conformity with Scripture, "that each one of us receives his own justice in the measure the Holy Ghost destines to each one (I Cor. 12:11) and according to each one's disposition and cooperation" (Denz. 799).

The "measure" of grace imparted to us is clearly said to be based on a twofold personal decision: on the one hand, God's free election in the Holy Ghost, when He grants grace as He pleases; and on the other hand, our cooperation with and through grace. Where God's decision is concerned, grace is imparted according to His good pleasure. In baptism and confirmation, each one of us receives God's formal assurance that such is really His mind in our regard. And we know that God has promised to give us grace in abundance. God's fidelity endures forever. Now, if God has chosen His elect and intends to keep them, it can only be owing to a still greater abundance of grace. For it would be blasphemous to suspect that a special election would in any way turn to our disadvantage. God's love for us is always far in excess of our love in return.

Intensity of grace, however, is also determined by our cooperation. But let us not imagine that this cooperation is patterned even distantly on the model of partnership among humans. To think so would amount to heresy, a form of Semipelagianism condemned in the fifth century. It is not at all as if God is committing to our care a large sum of money to which we, on our side, have now contributed a personal share—be it only a token contribution—that comes from us exclusively as our own. If this were the case, we would owe our eternal beatitude to ourselves. For while acknowledging that God has granted us grace in abundance, we would yet hold that it is we who, by our puny contribution, cause the divine loan to yield dividends. Some may take exception to the way we present this view on the ground that it smacks of financial calculations. But we can think of no more apt way to illustrate the quantitative notion of grace.

In point of fact, what is the truth concerning our cooperation in this respect? The truth is that whatever we give to God has been received by us from God. We give because it has been received. The only thing that is and must remain exclusively our own, as compared to what is from God, is sin or the principle of sin: the sloth, the tepidity, the unwillingness to let the divine grace triumph in us.

We take it, then, that grace increases according to God's free election. We know too that this election will, in any eventuality, surpass the measure of our ability to correspond; we cannot keep pace with God's love. Yet grace increases or decreases "according to each one's disposition and cooperation." When we freely consent to God's invitations, when we freely allow ourselves to be borne aloft by His grace, cost what it may in terms of effort and struggle—and that, too, is God's gift—then grace lives in us more intensely. But when we drag our feet, or worse still when we harden our hearts against the divine calling, forthwith the strength of grace is reduced. It lies within our power to block the flow of grace. Where grace wins through, it is certainly because of our cooperation, but still more because of God's love. We can never "glory in ourselves, but in God only" (I Cor. 1:29-31; Rom. 3:27, 4:2; Eph. 2:9; II Tim. 1:9).

In the next section we shall come back to the mystery of the divine election. Meanwhile, we should like to observe that, starting from another standpoint, we have reached a conclusion identical with the conclusion of our earlier discussion of God's presence: grace is a life of love from, in and through the divine indwelling. That life opens like a flower— *increase* is an unfortunate term—whenever we allow ourselves, in live faith and charity and therefore in personal surrender, to be taken up into intimacy with God. That life slows down, is stunted, whenever we go our own way, rely on self and abandon God. In this connection Trent quoted another of St. Augustine's pithy sayings: "God abandons no one unless He be first abandoned by him" (Denz. 804). Once again, this shows that there can be no question of grace increasing automatically by means of certain practices. He who would hold such a belief exposes himself to the danger of superstition.

The Problem of Election vs. Freedom

A few moments ago we made mention of one of the most difficult problems in the domain of grace. Not many decades after the Council of Trent, that problem monopolized practically the whole of the treatise on grace. The Dominicans and the Jesuits and later the Augustinians, followed still later by the Redemptorists, elaborated subtle systems of thought and strove with might and main to bring Rome to condemn or at least disapprove of the opposing party. The theological dispute struck the popular mind so deeply at the time that a "victory"—meaning here a disapproving decree from Rome—was an occasion for military parades, popular rejoicing and fireworks. Television did not exist in those days; if it had, it would have made capital out of the discussions and attracted as many spectators as an international football match does today.

In the end, several popes forbade the contending parties to condemn each other in future. Among them was Paul V, who on September 5, 1607, said that each religious order within the Church was allowed to keep its traditional system (Denz. 1090). We shall go no farther into these learned speculations except to say that in the course of time the conflicting positions showed signs of drawing a little closer to each other. Since the last war, most European theological faculties and seminaries have consigned all these systems to the museum of theological antiquities. No great loss to the reader. One thing seems clear: the single fact that so many sincere and intelligent thinkers discussed a problem with so much refining skill and subtlety without advancing one step closer to the solution of the problem is ample proof that the method followed during the debate was in all probability not the right one. So much for the reliance we can place on human reason.

For our part, we shall not come forward with a new solution purporting to clear up all difficulties. But we shall endeavor to indicate *why* no completely satisfying answer can be given. There are times when a theologian is in duty bound to be silent. We can do no better than to imitate the Church, which has been wisely discreet on this topic ever since the days of Augustine. One cannot but regret that this well-advised discretion has not been followed in the post-Tridentine period. Theological thought could have concentrated its energies more profitably on other problems, for instance, the pressing question regarding the relationship between uncreated and created grace. At any rate, the hopeless controversy is the reason the treatise on grace has remained one of the least satisfying parts of the whole of theology.

In the discussion below, we shall try to find out what is of faith in the two concepts, divine predestination and man's freedom under grace; and that will help us assess their religious bearing. In the next chapter, we shall try to confront these two truths with each other; and that will afford us an occasion to get to the bottom of the question, and to sense *why* we neither can nor may attempt to proceed any farther. Human reason left to itself must ever remain incapable of sounding the mystery of God's action.

God Remains First

What is of faith on the subject of divine predestination or divine foreordaining? The mere enunciation of these words sends up a red warning flag. It is not safe to try to synthesize the problem in such terms. For in God there is neither a before nor an after; there is only the eternal, unchanging now. Unhappily for us, we are unable to think without the help of our categories of time and space. We have no option but to content ourselves with using deficient words. Scripture could do nothing else, nor can the Church. But let us be warned.

We prefer to use a terminology that is less bound up with the succession proper to time. We prefer to speak of *God's primacy in grace*. But what does it mean?

Paul gave us the true meaning of that expression in the chapters which he devoted to the election of Israel. Paul was a Jew, and as Jew he suffered grievously at the thought that his own people had fallen out of God's favor. He asked himself the question, "Has God rejected His people?" (Rom. 11:1). And he replied, "God has not rejected the people which of old he chose for his own. . . . There remains today a remnant [the 'remnant' of which the prophets spoke], selected by the grace of God. But if it is by grace, then it does not rest on deeds done [in the observance of the Law]; otherwise, grace would cease to be grace" (Rom. 11:2-6). The Apostle repeated these thoughts when announcing the main theme of the Epistle to the Romans:

All alike [Jews and Gentiles] have sinned and have fallen off from the divine glory. And all are justified by God's free grace alone, through his redeeming act in the person of Christ Jesus. . . . He shows that he himself is just and that he justifies any man who puts his faith in Jesus. What room then is left for human boasting? It has been shut out. In virtue of what? In virtue of the good works in keeping the Law. By our own strength? No, but in virtue of the law of faith. And our argument is that a man is justified by faith apart from the observance of the Law. [Rom. 3:23-28]

At the close of our previous chapter, we referred to a whole series of Pauline texts taken from both the earlier and the later epistles, in which the same theme is consistently repeated. For example:

Brethren, think what sort of people you are, you called by God. Not many of you are learned by any human standard; not many are mighty; not many are highly born. To shame the wise, God has chosen what to the world is unwise; to shame what is strong, God has chosen what to the world is weak. God has chosen what is low and contemptible, things of no account, to bring to naught what is now in being, so that there be no room for human boasting in God's presence. It is thanks to him [the Father] that you are in Christ Jesus; for God made him to be our wisdom, our justification, our sanctification, our redemption; so that, as Scripture says [Jer. 9:22-23]: "If anyone boasts, let his boast be in the Lord."

As to what concerns my own person, brethren, when I brought the divine message to you, I did not come displaying fine words or learning [so highly prized among the Greeks, and not less among the Corinthians]. I had resolved to bring you no other knowledge than that of Jesus Christ, Christ nailed to the cross. I approached you with a distrust of myself, full of fear and trembling. My speech and preaching were not words of persuasive arguments of [Greek] wisdom; they carried conviction by the power of the Spirit; so that your faith might not be based on human wisdom, but upon the power of God. [I Cor. 1:26-2:5]

Such had always been the preaching of the old prophets; and Paul never deviated from it. To the Ephesians he wrote from his prison, "You owe it to grace that you have been saved through faith; not to yourselves, but to God's gift; not to any action of yours, so that no man might boast. For we are his work, created in Christ Jesus to do good works, which God prepared beforehand, so that we might live in him" (Eph. 2:8-9). From these words it ought to be plain that Paul was not condemning good works; he condemned only those on which we *pride* ourselves as if we performed them *by our own strength*. Toward the close of his earthly career, the Apostle wrote a last letter to his beloved disciple Timothy: "Take your share of suffering in the cause of the gospel, through the strength that comes from God. For it is he who has saved us and has called us to a life of holiness, not on the grounds of any work of ours, but because of his own purpose and his own grace" (II Tim. 1:9).

On January 25, 531, Pope Boniface II wrote a letter to St. Caesarius, Archbishop of Arles in France, to approve the resolutions passed at the local Synod of Orange as expressions of the true faith; the letter also contains a number of quotations from Scripture: "We rejoice that you, venerable brother, together with some bishops from Gaul, have judged the faith along truly Catholic lines. According to what you have written to me, you have unanimously defined that the faith, by which we believe in Christ, has been given to us by God's prevenient grace. To that you have added that nothing can be good in the sight of God unless man is enabled by God's grace to will this good, to begin this good and to accomplish it. Our Savior has said, 'Apart from me you can do nothing' (Jn. 15:16)" (Denz. 200b). This papal pronouncement is a fine expression of what we have called the primacy of God in grace. God is necessarily the source and goal of the stream of life which grace is for us.

Wrong Conceptions

But what exactly do we mean by God's primacy in grace? Our expression is founded on the basic truth of our faith that we are saved through grace and not through our own works, not through works which we can accomplish by our own strength. Not Paul nor any one of the Apostles nor the Church has ever denied that we must bend all our strength to doing the will of God, even in the midst of persecution. But that, too, is a grace, the fruit of God's election.

There is perhaps no truth over which we men of the West, and in fact all men, have been at more variance. The conflict began in the fifth century. A pious ascetic, Pelagius by name, a spiritual guide wielding considerable influence among the Roman aristocracy, began spreading a set of ideas which, after a long while, incurred condemnation by the Church. Augustine led the fight against Pelagius. It is indicative of the difficulty we have in realizing fully the fundamental Christian truth at stake that for many years the new ideas found support among the churches of both the East and the West. Even popes wavered long before censuring the new teacher. For one thing, Pelagius' intentions were almost surely excellent. For another, the question raised by Pelagius had not been gone into very deeply, Augustine said; and the Church was then at grips with another, more blatant heresy, Manichaeanism. Manes was not a Christian, but his doctrine greatly influenced the thought of the period. According to Manichaeanism, the body was evil and sinful, and came from the evil one. Only what was spiritual came from God.

As we have mentioned, Pelagius was an ascetic. Against Manes, he defended the soundness of the human will. God is no respecter of persons: He gives an equal chance to all men. We have to decide what our life will be, and we have the power to do so. If we were unable to do so, God could not in fairness reproach us with our failure, because it would be no fault of ours. Pelagius was prepared to admit the existence of some sort of grace. But this grace did not mean much in the main, for it consisted chiefly in the example and teaching of Christ. He may possibly have admitted more; but after so many centuries, and in the absence of documents, we cannot very well ascertain what it may have been.

Human nature, said Pelagius, has not been corrupted by original sin; and original sin is nothing more than the bad example of our first parents. That being so, children are not harmed by it and have no need of baptism. On this point, however, Pelagius later changed his mind, and came to accept that children should be baptized in view of heaven; but he maintained that they had no share in our common guilt. Pelagius intended, above all, to affirm the goodness of creation against Manes' teachings. God alone, and not the devil, created everything; and His work is good. Human will has remained sound. Otherwise God could not take us to account. The Pelagian doctrine, given here somewhat sketchily, died out long ago, though even today we may still hear some of the arguments it used.

The teaching was condemned by the Council of Carthage in 418. That Council stood under the leadership of Augustine, the "doctor of grace," as the Church would call him in later years. But the condemnation did not put an end to its history. It happened that St. Augustine went too far in stating some of his views. With the years, he spoke of God's election in terms all too pessimistic. That was enough to start another reaction, known later by the name of Semipelagianism. But what was Semipelagianism?

Some pious monks from Sicily and southern France considered the later works of Augustine to be rather hard, and they came up with another doctrine. What they taught concerning grace was richer than what Pelagius had had to say. Grace, they admitted, had truly to heal the consequences of sin within us. But we, too, had to contribute a share, in two ways, mainly. We have to take the first step toward God, very much as the sick man has to call the doctor, as the good thief had to beg to be remembered, and as Zacchaeus had to climb up in a tree before he caught sight of Christ. Second, from the moment we have received grace, we have to persevere in grace. That is *our* responsibility. And so, both the start and the terminus of the spiritual life are determined by our personal cooperation. God sees to the rest, and in the eyes of those pious monks that was a great deal indeed. They made use of the same arguments as Pelagius: God is no respecter of persons; He therefore takes account of what we do on our side, for otherwise He would be unjust.

We are confident that the reader experiences no difficulty in understanding the thinking of the Semipelagians. It is plain talk for men of common sense. They will be cheered by the knowledge that Augustine and Thomas Aquinas, the two outstanding theologians of the West, held similar opinions for a short while in their youth. Yet Semipelagianism was condemned in 531 by Boniface II when he approved the decrees of the Council of Orange in the letter quoted above; later, it was condemned solemnly by the Council of Trent.

Why is this doctrine indefensible? For this reason: if Pelagianism and Semipelagianism are right, then grace is no longer grace. Sanctity would be due to us, to our own personal efforts, to our own good works and not to grace; we would have a right to it. A moment's reflection will show this. If we hold that God has to rely on our cooperation, it follows at once that in the last analysis we owe faith and heaven to ourselves, to our personal cooperation.

The basic error of such a conception is that it looks upon the collaboration between God and man as taking place on the same level, as some sort of equal partnership; God and man would face each other on a par, and both would jointly have their part to play. The truth is not so simple. We have to affirm absolutely that God's contribution is far, even infinitely, in excess of ours. As long as we attribute anything, be it ever so little, exclusively to ourselves, we imply that this minimum of cooperation is the ultimate reason that we are saved. Even while granting that without God we would be incapable of anything, we would nonetheless be claiming that *we* are responsible for the final outcome. And this would empty the Christian message of grace of its innermost meaning.

An illustration might be of some use here. Let us suppose a mighty oil trust, disposing of an army of technicians and immense resources in machinery and capital. Let us suppose also a farmer on a small holding which happens to have oil. The man knows nothing about oil, and of course does not have the money to exploit it. He is asked simply to set his signature at the bottom of a paper placed before him by the lawyer of the oil trust. All that is required of him is a mere scrawl; but that signature will decide whether or not the oil brings any profit to his household. You will exclaim, "What a hopeless comparison!" Yes, undoubtedly; all comparisons are defective in some respect or other. But our example is not so lame as would appear at first sight. It illustrates the error in the theological notion outlined above: that in the last analysis God and man are assumed to stand on the same level. We shall have to come back to this initial error again and again, for it lies at the root of all the difficulties connected with the present discussion. Do what we may, our imagination persists quite unconsciously in setting God within the framework of human relationships.

What is defective in our illustration can be set right by courageously conceiving grace as we did above: grace is a living actuality, so intimately linked with the divine indwelling that it springs from, accompanies and leads to it. With this in mind, we shall think of God and man as standing not next to each other but *within each other*. We are surrounded, enveloped by His love.

We recall a personal experience of ours which happened in August, 1953, at the small Benedictine priory of Chèvetogne in the Belgian Ardennes. Several Protestants and Anglicans and some Russian Orthodox of Saint-Serge in Paris had come there to meet with Catholic theologians. The subject for debate that year was precisely the problem of grace. Evening was falling, marking the end of a busy day's discussion. Until that moment, only the Protestants and the Catholics had spoken. The Russians were plainly embarrassed. All our fine distinctions about grace were totally foreign to them. Someone inquired whether they had no contribution to make to the discussion. After a few moments of hesitation, Father John Meyendorff stood up. He is an expert in Byzantine patrology, and is at present a professor at St. Vladimir in New York.

"Well," he managed to say, "our Church, too, had to face this problem sometime in the twelfth century. At that moment Byzantium was having a revival of ancient Greek culture which would eventually spill over into your Renaissance. That pagan influence entailed some danger of Pelagianism. But our Church's reaction to it was very simple. We were in possession of the rich liturgy of the mass, which brings the living presence of the Blessed Trinity home to us. The Church did nothing more than remind the faithful of that heavenly life, begun by the reception of the sacraments. And that was quite enough."

There is much truth in Dr. Meyendorff's remarks. As long as we hold on to the genuine notion of grace, we shall meet with few problems arising from the Pelagianism still dormant in our culture. No sooner do we detach created grace from the living mystery of the divine indwelling than difficulties will crowd upon us thick and fast. For then we see grace no longer as a life *in* God but somehow as a life *before* God. And thus grace is misconstrued.

Freedom Under Grace

A serious question remains. It has plagued mankind ever since the author of the Book of Job composed his meditations on the sufferings in this world, ever since Paul wrote his Epistle to the Romans and spoke of the election and infidelity of the Jewish people. If what we have said so far is indeed the Christian doctrine, where does our freedom come in?

At this point it is customary in theology to present arguments purporting to explain the paradox. We shall not follow this custom. It is not to the advantage of a fruitful theology to strike a purely defensive attitude; the best apologetics will always remain the exposition of what is positive in the Christian message. Now, the message of grace is a message of freedom, the freedom of the children of God; yet few theological textbooks seem to say a word on the subject. He who looks upon the Church as a bulwark and a ghetto finds this message embarrassing. But to keep silent about it could be still more dangerous. Silence leaves the door wide open to a Christian variety of legalism, and we know Christ's mind on legalism.

Grace calls us to a new freedom, the true freedom. Scripture leaves us in no doubt about it.

In the New Testament we come across a conception of freedom which acknowledges the high esteem the Greco-Roman world had for the freedom proper to its citizens. The free man alone was reckoned to be fully human; not so the slave or the child (Gal. 4:1-7). It is strikingly noticeable that the idea of freedom appears seldom in the Old Testament. But some of the New Testament writers knew well the Greek conception of freedom and wanted to apply it to what is true freedom: freedom from sin. We were slaves of sin; now, however, we are all slaves of God, and are therefore free from sin (Rom. 6:6-23). We owe this gift of freedom to baptism (Rom. 6:6).

There is also a higher teaching about freedom in the New Testament, connecting it with the freedom of the Son and consequently of all those who share in his filiation. Matthew reported one of our Lord's sayings in which it seems to us that Christ mainly intended to indicate discreetly His divine sonship; but by the manner in which St. Matthew summed up the sequence of events, all of us are included in the freedom Christ spoke of:

When they [Christ and the Apostles] arrived at Capharnaum, the collectors of the temple tax came to Peter and asked: "Does your master not pay the temple-tax?" Peter answered: "Yes, he does." When he went indoors, Jesus forestalled him with the question: "What do you think, Peter: from whom do earthly monarchs levy tax or toll? From their sons or from aliens?" "From aliens," replied Peter. "Well then," answered Jesus, "the sons go free. But in order not to hurt the feelings of those people, go and cast a line in the lake; take out the first fish you hook up, open its mouth and you will find there a silver coin. Take it and make payment to them both for me and for yourself." [Mt. 17:24-27]

In the Gospel of St. John, we see how Christ gave a completely new connotation to the Jewish conception of freedom. And here, too, our new freedom is presented as linked with the freedom of the Son. Christ had just said, "You shall know the truth, and the truth will set you free." In John, truth is not abstract truth; it is the living word Christ preached, the message which He brought along with and in His Person. Truth is *par excellence* a concrete notion. And it is that doctrine which sets us free.

On hearing Christ's words, the Jews showed anger. "They replied: 'We are descendants of Abraham and have never been slaves to anyone. What do you mean by saying, "You will be set free"?' 'Indeed, indeed, I tell you,' said Jesus, 'he who commits sin is a slave.' " And now follows the idea of divine filiation: " 'The slave has no permanent home in the house, but the Son has his home forever in the house [of the Father]. If then the Son sets you free, you will indeed be free' " (Jn. 8:32-36).

To John such a freedom was an evident fact. It is established in us through the preaching of the Word of God, Who is truth and thus strength. It is brought to perfection in us by the Spirit. It confers upon us that Christian "frankness," the untranslatable Greek word *paresis*, meaning literally outspokenness, freedom in speech, self-assurance (see Eph. 3:1-2; Heb. 3:6, 4:16; I Jn. 2:28, 3:21).

Paul, Champion of Freedom

Paul is unsurpassed as the champion of Christian freedom. He defended it staunchly against the influence of some converts from Judaism who tried to impose the Pharisaic spirituality on the Christian community. Later as well, his self-assurance caused him many a hardship. It is possible to detect in the old manuscripts how the copyists tried to tone down some of Paul's more energetic expressions, very much as the *Osservatore Romano* censors papal speeches. "Prudent people" of this sort are to be found everywhere. They can speak of their religion only in pious, commonplace expressions, in "consecrated terms." Now, this sort of thing did not suit Paul's book at all.

Christians are not only free from sin (Rom. 6:12-23), from the flesh (Rom. 8:1-16) and therefore from eternal death (I Cor. 15:12-34). They are completely free from the Law. "Sin shall no longer be your master, because you are no longer under the Law, but under the grace of God" (Rom. 6:14). Exegetes have done their best to gloss over the Pauline affirmation. In their view, Paul had in mind only the ritual precepts of the Law abolished with the coming of Christian truth. But Paul meant all law, law understood even as the ethical expression of the natural law.

In Chapter 7 of his Epistle to the Romans, where he described the impotence of the Law to save men, he explicitly cited the command, "Thou shalt not covet," words taken from the ten commandments (Rom. 7:7; Ex 20:17; Dt. 5:21). According to one of our best Pauline scholars of today, Stanislas Lyonnet, the word *covet* never has a sexual connotation in the Septuagint Greek (that is, the classical translation of the Old Testament which Paul knew and used). Paul had in mind rather the nature of all sin: to want to be like God. Consequently, in citing that one commandment he summed up the whole law, as epitomized in the scene of paradise (Gen. 2:17).

Paul, no less than John, was well aware that love for God finds its expression in obedience to God's will, in the observance of the commandments: "Does this mean that we are to sin because we are no longer under the law but under grace? By no means. You know quite well that if you put yourselves in the service of a master, you are slaves of the one you obey; and that is true whether you serve sin, with death as its result; or obedience, with justice as its result. . . . Now, freed from the commands of sin and servants of God, you reap your fruit, an increase of holiness with its final result, eternal life. For the wages of sin are death, while the gift of God is eternal life in Christ Jesus our Lord" (Rom. 6:15-23).

He explained himself more clearly still in another passage: "You yourselves are our letter of introduction, . . . a letter coming from Christ, given to us to deliver, written not with ink, but with the Spirit of the living God"—here another image flitted across his mind, one borrowed from the Old Testament—"one written not on stone tablets, but in the hearts of living men. Such is our confidence in God, through Christ. Not that we are, of ourselves, competent and could claim anything as our own. What competence we may have comes from God. It is he who has made us competent ministers of the new covenant, a covenant not of the letter, but of the Spirit. The letter [the written law] brings death, but the Spirit gives life" (II Cor. 3:2-6). This text, too, indicates that the living, inner operation of the Spirit works out in us a deep trust, not in ourselves but in God. God's law has been written by the Spirit in our hearts, which means that from within it gives us the strength and the resolve to live up to the will of God in freedom. In our own language, we would say *to act on our conviction,* a conviction which has been given to us and yet is ours.

St. Thomas Aquinas, too, understood the scriptural text in that sense. We shall quote from him because many people betray some misgiving whenever there is question of freedom within the Church. We are not out to defend any "revolutionary" views of our own; we stand for a great tradition in the Church, the tradition of those who wanted to read Scripture and who dared to think in its light. The *Summa Theologiae* reads, "By the word 'letter' has to be understood any written law imposed on man from the outside, even the moral precepts contained in the Gospel" (I, II, q. 106, a. 2; see a. 1).

As we observed on a previous page, it would appear from the metaphors he used that Paul had before his eyes the prophecies of Ezechiel and Jeremias when composing his Epistle. Those two prophecies best describe the nature of grace as it was understood in the Old Testament.

Behold the days are coming, so says Yahweh, when I will make a new covenant with the house of Israel and with the house of Juda; not the covenant which I made with their fathers in the days I took them by the hand to bring them out of the land of Egypt. . . . But this shall be the covenant which I will make with the house of Israel, says Yahweh: I will give my law in their bowels, and I will write it in their hearts: and I will be their God, and they shall be my people. They shall no longer need to tell their neighbor, nor brother his brother: Learn to know Yahweh. For, all shall know me, from the least of them to the greatest, says Yahweh: for I will forgive their iniquity and I will remember their sin no more. [Jer. 31:31-34]

Ezechiel, in his turn, mentioned the same divine words and connected them with the messianic gift of the Spirit. After describing the sin of Israel which was punished with dispersal during the exile, Yahweh promised His forgiveness, not because of the merits of Israel but because of the sanctity of His name, because of Himself, out of pure, gratuitous grace.

Therefore, tell the house of Israel: Thus says the Lord Yahweh: It is not for your sake that I will do this, house of Israel, but for my holy name's sake [that is, God's Person], which you have profaned among the nations [the Gentiles] whither you went. And I will sanctify my great name, which is profaned among the nations; that the nations may know I am Yahweh, so says the Lord Yahweh, when I shall be sanctified in you before their eyes. I shall gather you [as a token of my grace] from among the nations [that is, from your exile] and I will bring you into your own land [the promised land]. And I will pour upon you clean water, and you shall be cleansed from all your filthiness and I will cleanse you from all your idols. And I will give you a new heart [for the Jews, the heart is the symbol of the deepest core of a person] and put a new spirit into you; I will take away the stony heart from your flesh and give you a heart of flesh [that is, a living heart]. And I will put my spirit in the midst of you [that is, in your innermost selves], and cause you to walk in my commandments and to keep my judgments and do them. And you shall dwell in the land which I gave to your fathers [image of the Church, the new people of God on earth]; and you shall be my people, and I shall be your God [the biblical expression to signify relationship between God and the people after the covenant]. And so will I deliver you from all your impurities. . . . [Ez. 36:22-29; see 11:19-20]

St. John, who owed so much to the prophets, declared unhesitatingly: "You have received from the Holy One an unction [that is, according to present-day exegesis, God's word given by Christ in the Gospel], and you know all things. I write to you now because you are ignorant of the truth, but just because you know it, and because from the truth no lie [no sin] can come." A few verses further on, he continued: "As for you, the unction which you have received from him abides in you, and you need no one to teach you; his unction [His teaching concretely presented as visibly revealed in Christ and as the power of His Spirit] teaches you everything; and that is true and no lie" (I Jn. 2:20-27). Christ Himself, during His life on earth, testified to the sanctifying strength of the word: "It is written in the prophets: And all shall be taught by God [Jer. 31:33; Is. 54:13]. Every one who has listened to the Father and has learnt comes to me. Not that anyone has seen the Father; he alone who is from the Father [that is, Christ only] has seen the Father. Indeed, indeed, I say to you: he who believes possesses eternal life" (Jn. 6:45-46).

Christ's living word, His truth, then, is an interior light and an operative force in our hearts. The Father employs it to teach us. That word is constantly revivified in us by the divine Spirit: "He will teach you all things and will recall to your minds whatever I have told you" (Jn. 14:25; II Cor. 1:21-22; Eph. 1:13-14). God's Spirit "will take away the stony heart . . . and give you a heart of flesh," so that we can keep God's commandments. Our face is no longer hidden behind the "veil" of the Old Testament, through which we can hear the word of God and yet not understand it: "Until now, when Moses is read, a veil lies upon their minds. But whenever anyone turns to the Lord, the veil is removed. For now the Lord is the Spirit, and wherever the Spirit of the Lord is, there is freedom" (II Cor. 3:15-17).

Liberty and Charity

Following in the footsteps of the prophets, neither John nor Paul denied that our holiness lies in our obedience to God's will. Obedience, however, is to be new and based on another law, the "law of Christ," which is His living word (Gal. 6:2; I Cor. 9:21), "the law of liberty" (Jas. 2:12; I Pt. 2:16; II Pt. 2:19), "the law of the Spirit of life" (Rom. 8:2).

In this light, we grasp the meaning of the charter of freedom which Paul addressed to his beloved Galatians. They were simple people, ex-servicemen who, after hard years in the service of the Empire, had been transplanted from Gaul (whence their name) to Asia Minor. During Paul's absence, they had been dangerously misled by the intrigues of Judaizing Christians who wanted to bring them over to the practice of circumcision and other Jewish observances.

Christ has set us free, to remain in freedom. Stand firm, therefore, and do not allow yourselves to be put again under the yoke of slavery [of the Law]. I, Paul, tell you: if you let yourselves be circumcised, Christ will be of no profit to you. Once again I declare: every man who lets himself be circumcised is under obligation to keep the entire Law. If you seek to be justified by way of the Law, you are severed from Christ, you are fallen away from grace. As for us, we hope to obtain justification through the Spirit and through faith. If you are in union with Christ Jesus, neither circumcision nor the lack of it has any meaning. What matters is faith, operative in love. . . .

Brethren, you have been called to freedom. Do not turn your freedom into license for your senses; but be servants to one another in love. For the whole Law is summed up in one commandment: Thou shalt love thy neighbor as thyself. . . .

This is what I mean: if you are led by the Spirit, you will not follow the desires of the senses. For the desires of the senses go against those of the Spirit, and those of the Spirit go against those of the senses. They are in conflict with each other, so that you do not do what you will to do. But if you are led by the Spirit, you are not under the Law. [Gal. 5:1-6, 13-14, 16-18]

Paul was to see his teaching concerning freedom put to a wrong use, especially by the Corinthians, his problem children. They fondly fancied that they had caught the Apostle's mind perfectly. They took for their motto, "To Christians all things are lawful." To this Paul replied, "Everything is lawful; yes, but not everything is harmless. Everything is lawful; but not everything is for the good of the others. Let no one seek his own advantage, but rather that of the others" (I Cor. 10:23-24).

Because of their new freedom, Christians were allowed to eat everything—unlike the Jews who, by the Law, were bound to some restrictions. Paul had nothing against Christians' eating the sacrificial meat which was sold on the market by the servants of the pagan temples, "For the earth is the Lord's and everything on it" (I Cor. 10:26). But in case they caused scandal to anyone by taking that meat, they had better, for charity's sake, renounce that freedom: "Whether you eat or drink, or do anything [Paul did not forsake his principle of freedom!], do it all for the glory of God. Give no offense to Jews, or Greeks, or to the Church of God. As to myself: I take as my rule to satisfy everyone, seeking the good of the others rather than my own, so that all may be saved. Follow my example as I follow Christ's" (I Cor. 10:31-11:1).

The one real danger that could beset such freedom is self-love, self-seeking. That is why freedom can be safe only where love is ruling, as in the case of Paul—or of Christ: "He who loves his neighbor observes all that the Law commands. For, all the commandments: Thou shalt not commit adultery, Thou shalt do no murder, Thou shalt not steal, Thou shalt not covet, and the rest, are summed up in this one saying: Thou shalt love thy neighbor as thyself. Love refrains from doing the neighbor any harm; that is why the whole law is summed up in love" (Rom. 13:8-10).

With almost hysterical enthusiasm, the Corinthians flaunted the visible and miraculous gifts of the Spirit: the gifts of prophecy, of ecstatic utterances, of tongues or languages. In connection with these, too, the one rule was: the good of the community, the edification of the others (I Cor. 14:1-19). And in the preceding chapter, Paul singled out the one gift which acts as a safeguard over all the other gifts of the Spirit, because it is the highest of them all— charity:

You should aim at the higher gifts. And I shall show you the best way of all. I may speak in tongues of men or of angels; but if I am without charity, I am no better than a sounding gong, or a clashing cymbal. I may have the gift of prophecy and know all hidden science: I may have such faith that I can move mountains [and no one has ever sung the glory of faith as Paul did]; but if I am without charity, I am nothing. I may give away all I possess to feed the poor [and according to the rabbis, this was a work by which one could gain extraordinary merit before God] and I may deliver up my body to be burned at the stake [even martyrdom, which should be the highest expression of charity]: but if I have no charity, it all goes for nothing. . . . Charity will never fail. The time will come when the powers of prophecy will stop, when speaking with tongues will come to an end, when knowledge will be useless. But charity will never fail. . . . Now three things persist, faith, hope and charity; but of these charity is the greatest. [I Cor. 12:31-13:3, 8, 13]

In charity alone does the message of freedom acquire its true significance. They both proceed from the same Spirit, and have been given to us by the Father in the truth, which is Christ, His living Word.

Liberty as Conviction

Let us reflect on this for a moment. Though it is no new doctrine, it is rarely spoken of. Most people, perhaps, do not dare reflect on it. We have heard laymen say, "We are Catholics; our bishops and priests do the thinking for us!" And this reminds one of Goethe's whimsical lines: "All wise things have been thought of already; all one can do is try to think them once more."

One point should be clear: God wants our hearts. No conformism, not even the most pious, can satisfy God's demand. Our hearts have been given to us in order that we may return them.

By the indwelling of the Father, we have become His children in the Son. God does not expect us to behave like strangers; He wants from us the affection of a child of the house. This affection is given us by the Holy Ghost. It is enough that we think along these lines to be constantly brought back to our basic understanding of what grace is: love.

Our status as children is our freedom as well, insofar as we act from conviction, from love. Love alone guarantees fully that this freedom will not lapse once more into the slavery of sin, which masquerades as freedom. It is plain from what we have seen on an earlier page, however, that as long as we live on earth, our freedom runs the risk of degenerating. But a risk never abolishes a right, or still less a duty. We are called to the liberty of children of God. This vocation of ours includes a divine demand. And that is the reason we may not keep silent on the subject of freedom. We have no right to do so. If we keep silent, we curtail and belittle the Gospel, Christ's message of salvation.

Law, the Guardian Leading to Christ

But then, what of the law? Did not God Himself give a law to the Jewish people? The Church, too, imposes on us divine and ecclesiastical laws in the name of Christ; and she reminds us that the laws of the land also oblige in conscience. That being the case, we Catholics land head over heels in a network of laws and precepts which seem to make serious inroads into our liberties, if they do not totally suppress them.

This objection may very well conceal a conception of freedom which has its roots not in the teaching of the Gospel but in the French Revolution and the age of liberalism.

For too many people, "to be free" means "to do what we please," and not "to become what we are." Freedom is not to be conceived of as directionless energy that can be made to serve life in any conceivable way. We truly exercise freedom only when we do from conviction what we must do, because we are what we are. Freedom in the service of evil, and thus used contrary to our deepest nature, is a thorough degradation of freedom. Evil-doing wounds and maims our freedom. We turn into slaves of sin; we become enslaved to self-will. Our freedom can blossom into a higher freedom by the practice of truth, and in no other way. Nonetheless, there is no escaping the impression that there is a multiplicity of laws which we as Catholics must take into account and conform to.

Of the old Law, Paul said that it "served the Jews as a tutor, bringing them to Christ to find their justification in faith" (Gal. 3:24):

This is what I mean: as long as the heir [the child of the house] is a minor, he is no better off than the servant, though all the estate is his; he remains under guardians and trustees until the date is fixed by his father. And so it was with us, while we were still minors, like slaves subjected to the elements of this world [especially the stars which, to the Greeks, were the ruling influence over human lives; among the "elements of this world," Paul ranked the Law of the Old Testament]. When the appointed time had come [as set by the Father], God sent his Son . . . to ransom those who were subjected to the Law, in order that we might become sons of adoption. To prove that you are sons, God has sent the Spirit of his Son in our hearts, crying: "Abba, Father." [Gal. 4:1-7]

Paul was obviously correct. Freedom, and more particularly Christian freedom, is not just a gift: it is a task. We must conquer freedom; or better, we must freely allow ourselves to be raised to a higher level of freedom. Like everything else belonging to human existence, our freedom has to mature, to become adult and grow in time. And this applies both to the individual man taken by himself and to human society or a nation.

As long as we are minors and remain immature, we need the external support of order and discipline. Moral immaturity may last a long time in some instances, despite progress on the technical, cultural or even intellectual level. And this, too, must be said of both individuals and society.

When all is said and done, the actuality of sin clings to us, preventing us from achieving a true adult age here on earth. Sin, together with its ensuing weaknesses, keeps us in the condition of minors; and in that state, we live with the permanent threat of being unable to put our freedom to unhampered use because of the allurements all around which lead us into temptations. As a result, none of us can really dispense with the external stimulus of a law acting on us as a "tutor" until Christ should come.

This reminds me of a conversation I had one day with a Latin American on the subject of freedom and of the obligation to hear mass on Sundays. "That is all very well," the young man remarked after some thoughtful moments, "but if for us there was no danger of committing mortal sin, we would not go to mass." Supposing matters were really so, we are dealing here with an unmistakably immature Christianity, as weak as that of a seven-year-old child who is still unable to grasp what the faith is all about. It would be nonsense to expect a child to act from conviction, at least in matters more or less above its understanding. Shall we not recall in this connection the words of Paul: "That is why so many among you are feeble and sick" (I Cor. 11:30)?

The Church's declaration that we are obliged under pain of sin to hear mass on Sundays does not make much sense if we see it as no more than a penal law or a traffic regulation, the transgression of which incurs the penalty of a given fine. By her declaration, the Church reminds us of our blindness regarding the vital significance of the eucharistic celebration on Sunday, the Lord's day. To convinced Christians, such a declaration is superfluous—as superfluous as the law of the Easter duties. It is a great pity that the Church should have to enforce on us our highest obligation by means of severe precepts. It all goes to show how far we are estranged from what Christian life ought to be, and how immature we still are.

We cannot do without laws; and this is because of our sinfulness. Paul himself did not hesitate to issue laws and apply them severely. Nor does the Church hesitate; nor have the founders of religious orders hesitated to impose laws on their members. All, though, have been convinced that precepts are no more than aids toward a nobler aim: the freedom that is ours as children of God.

Now, if the law is no more than the "tutor, bringing [us] to Christ," it is plain that its intention is uniquely to train us in the practice of true freedom. Those in charge of educating children both at home and at school ought to keep this in mind. It should also be remembered in the education of the Christian people in the parish, church organizations, religious orders and diocesan societies gathered around the bishop.

Most people in authority dread looking at things in this light. To them it seems far simpler—and more efficient—to set up and maintain a convenient façade by means of impersonal discipline. Grace, the indwelling of God, of the Holy Ghost—those are very fine ideas, but not to be relied upon in actual conduct. Here we have another instance of how latent Pelagianism breaks out into the open. Human administrative efficiency wants to manage things by means of unverifiable "inspirations."

Better perhaps than any other man in our age, Pope John XXIII gave proof of the persuasive power of trust in God and His grace, and of trust in the good will of men. We may safely say that his manner of acting has been a challenge to our times. It would have been quite easy for him to exercise his authority while the first session of the second Vatican Council was in progress; but he would have achieved much less if he had done so. We heard it said in Rome more than once: "This is nonsense"; "He is a positive danger to the Church." We are merely quoting.

The Law Is Spiritual

But the law is more than a prop to human weakness; "it is holy, just and good" (Rom. 7:13). "We know that the law is spiritual" (Rom. 7:14). *Spiritual* in St. Paul's vocabulary always means "inspired by the Spirit." The law is always an expression of the divine will. That was God's purpose when He established authority in the world and above all in the Church. "Who hears you hears me" (Lk. 10:16). The Apostles never hesitated to follow their mission, though they were conscious that it was a "service" and not the exercise of personal power. Our nature will always find it hard to come to know the will of God; it is the role of the Church to help us with motherly care, to enlighten and guide us in the discovery of the divine intention in our regard. And we believe that, in the exercise of her authority, the Church is led by the Holy Ghost. Authority, then, is truly "spiritual."

The question may be asked, does obedience, though a virtue, remain free? Or better perhaps, how does obedience make us free men? Let us first see what obedience does *not* stand for.

The law does not make free men of us when it is accepted *for its own sake.* We are not thinking now of an external conformity, for that is not true obedience. We are thinking of law considered as duty, and thus already more or less cut away from its root, which is the will of the living God. For the law would then contain its own perfection within itself; it would stand for definite human values in the cultural, social, national and even religious domains. To our minds, all these would somehow still appear related to God, but the emphasis would fall predominantly on the human performance, on fidelity to duty, on the sense of discipline, self-respect and solidarity with others.

These values should not be given primacy in our minds; otherwise a very dangerous process is bound to set in. First comes complacency in our own achievements; then we begin to compare what we have done with what others have failed to do. In no time we are esteeming ourselves as superior to the others, and then we look down upon them. From this consciousness are born the well-known categories among men, discernible already among children: we are the "good people," the others are the "wicked ones," the "evil ones."

What Paul described in such tragic terms in Romans 7 repeats itself all too often in the history of each man and of the Christian people. *Sin uses the law,* which may be able to tell us what to do but fails to give us the strength to do it, *in order to rule our lives again*—a very dangerous sin, indeed, in that it is next to impossible to unmask as sin, at least in the eyes of the people whom it affects. It is the sin of the "pious people."

In the end we assume a certain standing before God. We pride ourselves on our rights, on our "merits"; we hug our deeds to ourselves and trust that He, on His side, will take note of our achievements. "We are proud of ourselves, not proud of the Lord" (I Cor. 1:31). Before we realize it, we have wandered into undiluted legalism.

May we not say that this is the reason "virtue" is so often repelling? We have frequently asked ourselves why it is that "exemplary people" in religious communities or parishes fall short of our expectations and in the end do so little, while "unpredictable" types achieve much more. Far be it from us to state this as a law of the Medes and Persians; but that instinctive antagonism roused in us sounds an alarm: something is amiss. The one word suitable here seems to be *smugness*. Matters worsen when legal obedience develops into the kind of fanatical sectarian pride which of old blossomed into Pharisaism. This is a violation of what ought to be an authentic religious attitude. Christ's severe condemnation of such "pious folk" should ring in our ears forever.

We might draw profit from a most practical illustration. We have witnessed in our days the debasement of the noblest word in the Christian vocabulary: in some countries, one may no longer use the word *charity* for fear of evoking bitterness, even contempt and hatred. And this is due to a failure to understand the real import of the Christian message. It is quite easy, alas, to be "charitable" at the expense of others as a "practice of virtue"—our virtue, of course. But the very instant it amounts to that, charity is dead.

We have seen, then, how a legalistic attitude toward life can turn us into slaves of presumption and pride, and thus empty us from within of our freedom in grace.

Law, the Guidance of the Spirit

There is still another aspect of the law which we may not overlook. The law, more especially the written law, can hardly do more than trace a general outline of conduct for us. A law is always abstract; it never covers the living reality. Herein precisely lies its weakness. It may be true that a superior is in a position to judge the personal attitude his subjects ought to adopt in a given situation; but he is not entitled to absolve them from their own responsibility before God.

There is, assuredly, the trite qualifying clause, "where the

superior commands no sin"—a clause that never fails to be
quoted, and rightly so, but without added commentary.
There appears to be a supposition that in barbarian times
a rare superior could be found who would thrust a gun
into the hand of one of his subjects with the order to shoot
an enemy. That may indeed have happened in earlier centuries, as for instance when St. Charles Borromeo, as Archbishop of Milan, visited an abbey somewhere in the Alps
and was received with bullets from hot-blooded monks. It
is not very likely, however, that superiors these days would
be animated with anything reminiscent of Far West adven-
tures. But there are other "sins" of a subtler kind which
do not make for commendable obedience. Such are, for instance, dishonesty or forgery of documents, especially in
countries where a lax morality has permitted even clerics
and religious to hold that any sort of cheating of the gov-
ernment is legitimate as long as one is not caught. Women
superiors have to be on their guard in this respect.

We have in mind much more than all this. *Neither the
law nor a superior can absolve us from the personal responsibility we have before God.* We have to make God's
will our own. The divine will is as actual and real as God
Himself; and it includes obligations which no authority can
possibly foresee.

We must do our best to preserve that openness, that attentive attitude, that inner *disponibilité,* as the French like to
call it. God is a living God, addressing Himself to living
men and not to automatons. We must always look for this
personal guidance of God in our lives, within the framework of the precepts of the Church. That is the obedience
which sets us free.

A consequence might be that we will need to contribute
our strength to reforming the law or adapting it to modern
times, each one according to his state and calling. And this
is what is happening at the present moment when bishops,
priests and laity all over the world are endeavoring to make
a success of the Council. Each one of us has to remain
on the alert for God's voice speaking in his inner soul;
each one has to show a genuine *paresis,* an undaunted Christian assurance, even when domineering and clerical-minded
authorities do not favor it or indeed are dead set against
it. It is a completely wrongheaded notion to say, as did a
Roman prelate in the course of a press conference, that
the laity and priests have nothing else to do during the

Council than await the decisions of the bishops. There is no need to mention here that the bishops alone, in communion of faith with the pope, have the authority to decide on the reforms needed in the Church; but nonetheless, the undertaking is a matter which concerns the whole Church. No authority in the Church can deprive or relieve us of the responsibility we have to God. And this is what confers upon our obedience its high value of freedom and spiritedness.

The main intent of each one of us must be to discover the will of God in his life. This supposes at least an elementary acquaintance with what is called the *discernment of spirits*. The Holy Ghost speaks to us in our lives, in our hearts. And we have to learn to discern His voice. But who teaches such Christian wisdom to the laity or to the priests?

It has become commonplace to say that Ignatius Loyola was the protagonist of iron discipline. Even outside the Church, many have ready at hand the celebrated quotations, *"perinde ac cadaver"*—"as if he were a dead body"—and "like an old man's staff." Nothing is surprising in this. Ignatius had been a military man; quite naturally, he has been consigned to the appropriate category of professions.

It is unlikely that soldiers were drilled during his lifetime as are our commandos today. And it would be a cheap anachronism to picture Ignatius as a Prussian sergeant-major or a British sergeant of the guard. However, as he wanted the practice of obedience to be the distinctive mark of his Society, it is worthwhile to see his real mind on the subject of this virtue.

In his *Constitutions*, he not only lent his legislation an exceptional suppleness by the added qualification "as far as is possible," but he linked his rules with the immediate guidance of God by frequently repeating the phrase, "according to the measure of the unction of the Holy Ghost." The ultimate rule of conduct he left to religious formed by years of prayer and study is the *discreta caritas*, a wise and prudent love for God. His *Spiritual Exercises* teach the retreatant how to listen to the voice of the Holy Ghost, how to tell inspirations from the moods and whims of the human heart. No one understands the nature of Ignatian spirituality unless he sees in it an alert openness of the mind vis-à-vis the inspirations of the Holy Ghost. It is useless to look in Ignatius' teaching for the "No arguing, please" of

Frederick the Great. An obedience descending upon us vertically from on high is a caricature of Christian obedience.

Conclusion

Grace is love, and therefore freedom; only in this setting can we claim to practice authentic Christian obedience. Naturally, this makes obedience all the more weighty. It is far easier to leave others the task of making decisions and to settle down safely and comfortably in a smooth, rule-bound existence. God is unsafe and uncomfortable. He treats us not as mental weaklings but as free men in whom freedom is a reflection of His glory. Christianity means responsibility and daring, the courage to live and act freely. It is no reformatory for straying teenagers.

We have seen how grace endows us with freedom, and how this freedom reaches its maturity in obedience. In the earlier centuries of the Church, this was so manifest to all that the word *libertas* was chosen to designate the freedom which grace bestows on us. Whenever natural freedom came under consideration, the words *liberum arbitrium* were used.

We end this part with Canon 25 of the Synod of Orange, which put a stop to the Semipelagian controversies; the felicitous phrases sum up all we have said about God's primacy in grace and about freedom: "To love God is an absolute gift of God. He Himself gave us the capacity to love Him; He Who is unloved loves us. When we were as yet displeasing to Him, we were loved, so that the possibility of pleasing Him might arise in us. For He poured out into our hearts the Spirit (Rom. 5:5) of the Father and the Son, Whom we love with the Father and the Son" (Denz. 198).

The Relationship Between Election and Freedom

The following discussion on how to combine the divine election and our personal freedom runs the risk of remaining on a purely academic level as long as these two truths have not been sharply delineated, as we have attempted to do above. Regarding their relationship, someone may ask whether we have an answer to the objection from reason: if it is God Who works out through grace whatever is good in us, how can we be free?

Faith has already provided us with the main answer. If grace is indeed love, then it means freedom. There is nothing so personal, so spontaneous, so free as love. Love is the soul of freedom. But we are able to grasp this only when we do not conceive of grace as a "thing" in us, some sort of directionless energy. Neither may we think of it apart from the divine indwelling. Grace originates from the indwelling, is bred in the indwelling and leads to a more complete indwelling. Grace signifies the personal relations of love.

A number of difficulties spring from the fact that we speculate about God's moving power as if it were an object. We speak in images borrowed from the material world. When I give a push to a carriage, the carriage *has* to budge. When I am given an injection, my fever *must* come down. When I switch on the light, darkness *cannot* remain. In the parable with which we began our study of grace, the girl stayed free because the young man had won her through love, and not through violence and chains.

St. Augustine endeavored one day to bring these truths home to the simple folk of Hippo. He was commenting upon the Johannine text, "No man can come to me unless the Father, who has sent me, draws him. . . . Everyone who has heard of the Father and has learnt, comes to me" (Jn. 6:44-45). It is one of Augustine's finest texts; we hear in it the saint, the theologian and the astute ob-

169

server of the human heart. All priests read this passage every year in their breviary during the octave of Pentecost.

"Do not think that you are drawn against your will; the mind is drawn by love. . . . If it was right for the poet to say, 'Everyone is drawn by his own pleasure' (Virgil, *Ec.* 2)—not necessity, therefore, but pleasure, not obligation but delight—how much more boldly ought we Christians to say that man is drawn to Christ when he delights in truth, delights in blessedness, delights in justice, delights in life everlasting, all of which is Christ?"

Suddenly, Augustine appealed to the experience of his audience: "Give me one who loves, and he understands what I say; give me one who longs, give me one who hungers, give me one who is traveling in this wilderness and thirsting and panting after the fountain of his eternal home; give me such a one, and he knows what I mean." Farther on, feeling powerless to express himself adequately, he has recourse to homely illustrations well within the understanding of the people of Hippo: "Hold out a green branch to a sheep and you draw it. Nuts are shown to a boy and he is enticed; he is drawn by what he runs to, drawn by loving it, drawn without hurt to the body, drawn by the bonds of the heart. If then these things, earthly delights and pleasures, have the power to attract when shown to those who love them, since it is truly said, 'Everyone is drawn by his own pleasure,' does not Christ, as revealed by the Father, attract us?" (*Joan. Evangel.* 26, 4; P.L. 35, 1608).

God Reaches the Heart

We are now able to enter more deeply into the subject matter. And this will afford us the opportunity to throw light on still another aspect of grace and to correct a widespread misconception.

We are thinking here of the *supernatural* character of grace, about which much has been written these last twenty years and which has been the source of frequent misunderstandings. Augustine's text sets us on the right road. The value proper and peculiar to love is that it moves us to act from within the innermost core of our own person. It is *our* action, though it is at the same time God's gift.

When and how can it be said that violence is done to our

freedom? Whenever coercion is brought to bear on us from outside, whenever something is forced upon us by physical might or, more subtly, by psychological pressure or moral constraint. Coercion injures the nobility of freedom because it violently assails the autonomy of the human conscience and person. In other words, the normal exercise of my autonomous human activity, befitting my human dignity, is trespassed upon. Normally, man acts from his own conviction and pursues his own object. We do not deny the influence of the numerous determining agents our earthly life is subjected to; in the last resort, however, it is the responsible person who makes a choice from the given possibilities. Whatever the nature of the violence used, it trespasses upon the normal exercise of my activity; it moves upstream, so to speak, and seeks to reach the very source of my action, my personal conscience.

Love never coerces. *Nor does God.* Man somehow makes exception here, insofar as we are all extraneous or foreign to each other. A man has no real power over the freedom of another man. He cannot reach it; he cannot get a grip on it. To win another man over to his views, he is compelled to employ external means. The discretion he uses according to the occasion may prevent him from interfering with the freedom of the other, and may make him attempt to persuade the other rather than coerce him. But he cannot succeed in persuading the other without a minimum of importunity. Ruysbroeck puts it very neatly: one man works upon another man from outside inwards, but God alone comes to us *from within outwards.*

We have had several occasions to lay bare the root error in our manner of conceiving grace, which is that the imagination induces us to look upon God as upon someone standing on a level with us, like a partner. The experience which ministers to our thinking process has never disclosed to us any other form of "influence." We spontaneously see God's sanctifying action in the light of our human experience; in other words, we think of it in terms of the way one man acts toward another. Nor can we perhaps ever escape completely from this mode of thought. And that is why we should be mindful of this defect whenever we deal with grace. We should imitate the astronomer who knows the structural defects of his telescope and takes them into account in all his calculations.

Let us take another example, one that illustrates strikingly how hard it is for anyone to get out of himself in order to see the behavior of another as it really is. Very few people are able to watch the perplexing and often unpleasant reactions of a mentally weak person and judge them objectively without displaying at once impatience and vexation and without passing moral judgments which are perfectly pointless under the circumstances. A sick man, too, may have "selfish" reactions that have little in common with egotism properly speaking. We behave in a similar way in our dealings with beings of an order lower than ours. We instinctively attribute to the behavior of animals, and today even to electronic machines, a human content they cannot possibly possess. Now, just as we raise this lower world to ours, so quite unwittingly we lower the divine action to our level. We are not much better than the pagans who looked upon their gods as supermen and attributed to them their own passions, defects and virtues, though in higher degrees. The world of Olympus was a reflection of our own human existence, but intensified to the fantastic heights of mythology and fable.

In order not to be misled, we must constantly correct our instinctive way of conceiving God's working in us. God is not standing *outside us,* as one like us; He is *within us.* In the words of St. Augustine, He is *intimior intimo meo,* far more interior to us than we are to ourselves. God is thus interior precisely because He is so totally different from us—because He is the "absolutely other," totally unlike us in being, sanctity and justice—and also because He is equally so totally beyond us. In philosophical language we could say that the absolute measure of His transcendence indicates to us the equally absolute measure of His immanence.

God, then, does not work in us from the outside, violently imposing Himself on us, binding and determining us to do what is good. As Creator, He stands at the wellspring of our existence, at the point where it flows uninterruptedly from His creative hand. He alone can reach our freedom right at its source and yet do it no violence. On the contrary, He renews it and endows it with true freedom. To understand this well, we should keep in mind that freedom is inseparably bound up with truth, or, as the saying goes today, with authenticity. We must freely become what in fact we are. God does that for us by His grace. Any other sort of freedom must necessarily be an enslavement to self.

Nature and Supernature

We can elucidate this in yet another way, and it will afford an occasion for clarifying our understanding of the supernatural character of grace. An exact insight into grace is of decisive importance for us to build up an authentic Christian spirituality. We shall attempt to explain what is supernatural in grace by means of a threefold dialectical movement which takes into account all the various aspects of that living reality.

As a first step, we discover grace to be a *pure gift,* a complete surprise. The very revelation of grace acquaints us with this real element: ". . . or grace would cease to be grace" (Rom. 11:6). Grace is a pure gift because it is given to sinners, to men unworthy of it. And it is still more so because it lets us share in the inner life of the Blessed Trinity, which lies absolutely beyond our reach unless God lifts us up to it. In actual truth, we are already now standing in and with the Son as children before the Father through the power of the Holy Ghost.

No sooner have we said that much than we have to qualify our wording. Our imagination automatically associates the notion that grace is a totally new life with another idea —that if it is new, it is no longer a "human" life, but verges perhaps on the nonhuman. To some people, *super*nature seems to convey the meaning of *un*natural. And this, too, is false.

However much we emphasize that grace remains the supreme surprise for our nature, we have to affirm with equal force that grace sets our deepest humanity free, precisely because it restores our most authentic humanity to us and by this means *humanizes* us to an eminent degree. This is the second step in our dialectical movement.

As Father Piet Schoonenberg puts it, by grace we *are what we are given to be.* "We could express it differently: what we receive from God, we do not exactly possess, but we are it." [23] Properly speaking, we do not receive grace; we do not

[23] Piet Schoonenberg, *Het geloof van ons Doopsel* ("The Faith of our Baptism") (4 vols., 's Hertogenbosch: L. C. G. Malmberg, 1955-1962), III, p. 251.

possess it as something foreign to us, or as something entering into us from outside; but *we are our grace*.

Many novels and plays have been written to try to disentangle the ambiguity latent in a gift. Everyone endowed with average discernment sees that of its nature a gift is a "symbol" of esteem, of love. It has a role peculiarly its own in maintaining personal relations between men. For all that, it does not escape the observant mind of some thinkers that a gift also has its shadows. It obtrudes itself on us; it imposes obligations on us; it is a threat to our freedom; it may even be humbling. Alms and a gift lie only a hair's breadth apart. And so some people might look upon grace as a threat to their autonomy, as a divine importunity.

Such a notion is not correct. What we receive, as a purely gratuitous gift, is at bottom our own self. We do not speak here of God's creative act but specifically of the divine activity of grace. Grace is "a new birth" (Jn. 3:7), a "new creation" (II Cor. 5:17; Gal. 6:15). Ezechiel and Jeremias spoke of a "new heart" (Jer. 31:33; Ez. 11:19, 36:26). We know today that in Hebrew *heart* is used not so much as a symbol of love but rather as a symbol of the core of our personality. From grace there arises in us a new "I." In God *we are* what we receive.

To unveil yet more of the rich treasures contained in this view, we can do no better than contemplate, with Father Schoonenberg, the mystery of the incarnation. We discover the highest exemplar of grace in the intimate union of Christ's humanity with the Person of the Word. The grace which is ours is but a reflection of the ineffable grace which accrued to the Man Christ in the incarnation of the Son. We share in that grace in a limited and created degree; but further, the meaning of this supreme grace sheds light on the meaning of our own grace. To the Christ Man too, the union with the divine Person Who took to Himself that humanity is a sheer, gratuitous grace, though in this concrete instance (that is, if we consider the living Christ Who is unthinkable apart from his union with the Word) we could perhaps risk speaking of a right of Christ's. As we can see here too, at every turn we discover that our notions are limited and unfit to express the ineffable without deforming it.

What was the effect produced in Christ by the singular union between the second Person of the Blessed Trinity and the sacred humanity? This: that Christ was the most excellent of men. We often think of Him quite differently; we do not find it easy to think of Christ as a man. We are constantly tempted to surround Him with the phantomlike luster of the superman. The apocryphal writings, dating from the first centuries of the Christian era, succumbed to this temptation. They deal in fables. The high value of the true Gospels lies precisely in the fact that they do not do that.

Father Schoonenberg ventures upon a paradoxical sentence: "In Christ, His divinization was His humanization." [24] Because of the intimate union between the Christ Man and the Godhead of the Word, the Man grew more intensely man and human. The reason for saying this is, once again, that God does not reach us from outside but from within, from inside the very ground of our existence, from inside the intensity core of our person, from inside our "heart"—and all *because* He is the "totally other."

*Super*natural does not at all mean *super*human, and still less *non*human—at least, not in the sense of suggesting that grace either destroys the human values or throws them into the background. On the contrary, they acquire a new significance and worth.

In the spirituality commonly met with in convents and religious writings, a distinction is drawn between the purely natural human values in our life and the "supernatural" ones. The natural values are treated as having little or no consequence unless they are sanctified by a special "good intention," which has to be *superimposed* on them. The joy of watching a glorious sunset has no supernatural value unless I offer it up to God. A mother loves her children—but that is normal. A man goes to his office—but that is as it should be. I am polite and tactful in dealing with others—but the contrary would be unthinkable. If these activities and states are to have any value before God; more especially, if there is to be any "merit" in them in the sight of God, something must be added, namely, a "good intention." A little more and these people would declare that nothing but the exceptional, the uncommon, counts for anything in God's eyes. Hence they embrace a constrained spirituality that is not met with in the life of Christ or in the lives of most saints.

Of course, this is a wrong notion of the supernatural, the spiritual. The Germans have a name for it: the doctrine of

[24] *Ibid.*, p. 139.

the two stories. On the ground floor are the service quarters, on the top the drawing rooms. God does not deign to appear on the ground floor; He dwells only in drawing rooms! The truth is that our divinization is also our humanization. We have been made children of God in a renovated humanity. God is pleased with our courtesy to others as much as with our prayers, with our enjoyment of nature as much as with our rejoicing in His glory, with our human friendships as much as with our faith, with our justice and loyalty as much as with our charity—so long as we act *with the heart of a child of God*. No special intention is required for the purpose. We shall come back to this aspect of grace in Part III of this book, where we deal with grace as a new and authentic form of humanism.

Undoubtedly—and here we come to the third step of our dialectical movement—sin, our deep-seated pride and self-love remain tragic realities in our lives. Therefore, the humanism given to us by grace has to be protected by grace against the self, the "lower self" which "sees the good I want to do, but fail to do" (Rom. 7:19). While on earth, our Christian humanism can never achieve complete harmony or our powers perfect integration. Our earthly home is the place of our mortification, of our penance, of self-discipline, of asceticism and spiritual combat. However, the human in us as such is not the source of sin; nor is the body, for that matter. Spiritual pride alone upsets the balance between our bodily and spiritual endeavors and causes the body to turn into a temptation—as happens, for instance, in sexual life.

This being granted, we do not object to the practice of "good intentions"; but we are not in favor of the artificially added "special intentions" where these do not rise spontaneously. We mentioned earlier that the noblest of Christian virtues can be made into a caricature by such nonsense: we "practice charity" at the expense of our neighbor, for God's sake! The saints have not insisted on the necessity of "special intentions"; they have stressed the need of *purifying* our intentions. This is a different thing altogether. As long as the human in us, though reborn through grace, remains beset by the danger of self-love, our fundamental orientation from within is threatened with the risk of swerving away from God. That is why we have to purify our intentions. To redress our sloth, our *pesanteur humaine*, our human sluggishness, we must renew our intentions as the occasion requires, and at the same time refocus them on God. A child does not need to repeat constantly that it loves its parents. Yet a child acts sensibly when it renews its affection, so to say, in appropriate circumstances. And this applies equally well in the spiritual life.

God loves us *as we are*. He calls us to Himself *wherever we are*. He does not disavow His initial creative act by infusing grace into us; rather the contrary. His purpose is not to turn us into something quite different, something that would be neither angel nor man. As the French put it, with good reason, *"À vouloir jouer l'ange, plusieurs ont fini par jouer la bête"*—"Many who have wanted to act like an angel have ended by acting like a beast."

A pernicious spirituality of this sort has wrought havoc in many religious houses and has destroyed several vocations. Above all, it has thrown discredit on Christianity itself and has exposed both piety and virtue to odium. We all feel in our bones that something is amiss in such an attitude, that dangerous illusions have crept in. Unfortunately also, this attitude has made it impossible to build up a sound spirituality for the ordinary layman. It implies that a layman cannot aspire to holiness unless he somehow renounces his normal human joys and obligations, that he must borrow something from the monastic life or else he will stay hopelessly caught in the toils of mediocrity. But all this is nonsense. A mother sanctifies herself by fully living up to her motherhood. A father sanctifies himself by assuming his masculine responsibility both at home and in his work. Friendship, all too often frowned upon in religious houses and educational institutions, is no obstacle to sanctity unless it ceases to be friendship and becomes two-person egotism.

We see from our threefold dialectical investigation that grace is purely and gratuitously grace and at the same time the finest unfolding of ourselves, for the reason that God reaches us in the depth of ourselves. If abnegation and penance are necessary, it is not because we are not allowed to be men but because we are *sinful* men. Let the reader go over the text previously quoted from the Council of Trent on the subject of merit; he will see for himself that the Church has expounded the notion of merit along the lines of the same three aspects we have presented. Grace has nothing foreign about it. Sin alone is inhuman; that is why it is so monotonous.

What Election Is Not

We hope that our considerations have brought home the idea that through grace God raises and refines our freedom and even humanizes it. All the difficulties, however, are not yet out of the way. Our faith speaks of grace; but it also speaks of election and predestination. The question now is, what becomes of our freedom in the context of that election and that predestination?

Our first answer will consist in proposing a purer understanding of this mystery, in ridding it of a variety of false notions.

Before the actual shooting of a film, the screenplay is written out in full and set down in a book called the script. Each individual scene is described: lighting, sound, camera angles, décor, costumes, location, interplay of actors, dialogues—in short, whatever has any importance for the shooting of the film. The script girl is entrusted with the specific task of seeing that the script is faithfully followed in all its details. Now, if we think of God as acting along analogous lines, we can imagine that from all eternity He has prepared the script of our human history. The angels would be the script girls, carefully watching that no detail marked in the book is passed over. And then, naturally, we ask ourselves, how can we be free if everything is "written in the book"? The passivity with which many Mohammedans undergo their lives of poverty, giving no thought to seeking any improvement, is to be ascribed to their belief that everything has been "written in the book" beforehand. Similar fatalistic sects have been known to exist in Christendom.

We warned the reader earlier against the defective manner of thinking hidden in such a representation of reality. In God, there is neither a "before" nor an "after"; there is simply an eternal "now." Of course, we are unable to form an adequate idea of this divine condition. Do what we will, the category of time intrudes itself on our thought.

Sufficient and Efficacious Grace

Before going deeper into this matter, we should like to present in their correct form a couple of theological notions that came into general use toward the second half of the seventeenth century. During the Jansenist controversy, it became fashionable to distinguish between two kinds of grace; this distinction has eliminated a great deal of work for theologians. Most readers have probably heard of what are called sufficient grace and, still more celebrated, *gratia efficax*. One could translate the latter by "effectual grace," "infallible grace" or "grace achieving its end." But each one of these translations touches upon only one aspect of the original idea. Let us call it "efficacious grace," as is customary. In case the reader has never come across these terms in the past, we advise him to skip what follows and to pass on immediately to the next part of the book. He will miss nothing that was not said before. Experience has shown that many of the laity and priests are vexed by these hapless notions, and this is the only reason we have decided to write something on the subject.

To understand how those notions came about, we should have an idea of what Jansenism taught. On hearing the word *Jansenism,* most people think of an austere moral teaching dissuading the faithful from frequent communion. Jansenism began as a theology of grace and of man. Man, it said, is radically vitiated by original sin, so much so that when he succeeds in avoiding one particular mortal sin, he inevitably falls into another mortal sin, be it only the sin of pride. Moral corruption reaches such depths in human nature that even the just are incapable of keeping some of the commandments, notwithstanding the help of grace. To perform a good action, man needs an "irresistible grace," called after Augustinian terminology *delectatio bona victrix,* an "overwhelming attraction to the good," which necessarily overcomes our inborn inclination toward evil. Those who receive this grace are the elect of God; everyone else is rejected by God. Considering that God has no obligation whatever toward men, He may leave them in their sin if He pleases.

The Church has condemned the Jansenist doctrine, especially the three following propositions. (1) "Some of God's commandments are impossible for the just who wish and strive to keep them [considering the abilities they actually have]; the grace by which these commandments may become possible is also wanting." (2) "In the state of fallen nature, no one can ever resist interior grace," which means that grace, when given, is irresistible. (3) "To merit or to demerit [that is, to sin] in the state of fallen nature, it is enough to be free from external coercion but not [internal] necessity" (Denz. 1092-1094). Everyone realizes the fatalistic nature of such a doctrine of grace, which solves the problem of man's election in such gloomy terms.

The Church could not but condemn those propositions. They run counter to the data of faith. They were solemnly defined as heretical by Pope Innocent X, and this was confirmed by Pope Alexander VII (Denz. 1098). Let us observe that the pope concerns himself only with *factual* relations; for the faith is above all about *facts*. To put it differently, it is a *fact* that in the state of fallen nature, that is, the actual state in which we have our existence, God always gives *sufficient* grace to keep His commandments.

Besides this, theology has rightly taken into account the further fact that our freedom becomes true freedom only by growing and developing. Theologians correctly point out that sufficient graces do not deliver us at once from committing this or that sin, but supply at least the help we need to dispose ourselves gradually by prayer and mortification to genuine and complete obedience. All this is fully understood. God deals with us as we are. Freedom has been entrusted to us as a task. We must freely mature into a full freedom. Thus, the notion of *sufficient grace* acquires a more dynamic meaning, in accordance with experience and with the teaching of the saints.

The Church has defined nothing about actual grace, except that in no case may it be looked upon as "irresistible." Man always retains the possibility of rejecting grace; and this Jansenism denied.

The teaching of the Church is plain. Theology, however, "reified" that teaching to such an extent that for a long period it caused more headaches than comfort. What was the reason for this? As we have said repeatedly, grace had been cut away from the indwelling. Interest in sanctifying grace was on the wane; consequently, there had to be trouble.

It soon became common practice to apply the teaching about sufficient and efficacious grace to actual grace. Inevitably, this led to a blind alley. For if one starts by looking upon sufficient grace as a thing all its own, an isolated entity, one logically concludes that whenever man fails to accept that grace, "sufficient grace" changes into a "purely sufficient grace." By sheer necessity, one lands in the paradox that what was "sufficient grace" proves to be in fact an "insufficient grace," considering that sin has been committed in spite of it. It is easy to understand why the Jansenists made fun of this grace and parodied the invocation in the litanies of all saints, "From all sufficient grace, deliver us, O Lord," an invocation which could not be tolerated. It was condemned by the Holy Office on December 7, 1690 (Denz. 1296).

The censure was correct, of course. But it is nevertheless possible to caricature "sufficient grace." What the Church has solemnly defined is that when we sin Almighty God cannot be blamed for it. We alone are at fault, since God's help is sufficient to avoid sin. The substance of this is that we should never speak of an isolated sufficient grace, but rather of grace being sufficient or adequate. We will then steer clear of wrong conceptions. In fact, that is all the faith tells: that God's grace is always sufficient—or better, superabundant.

The same misadventure befell "efficacious grace." No pope, no council has ever defined efficacious grace to be an article of faith. The term, however, contains a real meaning for the faith, and does not suggest the idea of an actual grace isolated and standing by itself, something which achieves its end by itself. Otherwise we adopt a position hardly different from the erroneous notion of the Jansenists, who accepted the existence of "irresistible grace." Dogmatically, in terms of faith, *efficacious grace* can mean only one thing: whenever a man performs a good action, acceptable in the eyes of God, he owes it in the last analysis to God. Here, too, we shall be well advised not to speak of efficacious grace as a thing apart, but rather to speak of *God's primacy in grace* manifesting itself in my good deed. And this brings us face to face once more with the problem we are discussing.

It is clear now that we can safely write a theology of grace without entering into the relatively recent theological speculations about the mechanism of a separate sufficient grace and a separate efficacious grace. We like to stress this point, for experience has shown us how confusing such notions can be.

In her declarations, the Church has never proceeded farther than what she settled in earlier times concerning the difficult problem of our election. We may illustrate this by turning to the controversy in the ninth century over the subject of divine election through grace. A local synod at Quiercy-sur-Oise, France, gave an answer in the year 853 which accurately sums up the fundamental, factual truths of our faith on the question. The answer is valuable mainly because it aptly brings together many former declarations of popes and councils: "We lost our free will in the first man; but Christ our Lord restored it to us. We possess a free will to do good insofar as grace goes before and helps it; and we possess a free will to do evil insofar as grace abandons it. The will we have is free because grace has freed it and has healed it from corruption." The next canon after this considers the same mystery in the wider perspective of God's salvific will, while correcting a few less felicitous expressions occurring in the preceding canon: "Almighty God wants all men without exception to be saved (I Tim. 2:4), though not all are actually saved. The fact that some are saved is due to the gift of Him Who saves; the fact that some are lost is to be blamed on them that are lost" (Denz. 317-318). Please notice that the synod deliberately stopped on the threshold of the mystery, and did not propose more than what we, in the course of these pages, have discovered in Holy Scripture.

Election and Indwelling

Is it possible to go one step farther? We are probably authorized to consider the mystery from a closer view, but it must be in the light of the divine indwelling as we have expounded it. In the living presence of God, our person is taken up into the intense life of love proper to the Blessed Trinity; as a result, there arises in us an urging of grace to love God ever more and more. In this setting, to speak of "sufficient grace" or "purely sufficient grace" makes little or no sense, unless one chooses to limit himself to the meaning these terms had during the Jansenist controversy. Grace, seen as coming down from God to us, cannot be other than a divine superabundance. All limitations in the stream of God's grace are due to our ill will and sin, as was pointed out before.

When we are careful to take into account the appeal God addresses to us through the indwelling, we might, if needed, speak of "actual grace." But we shall have a more correct view if we speak of God's primacy in grace. God's primacy in grace is unmistakably evident when we place ourselves within the framework of the personal relationships we are able to discern in the divine indwelling. But all becomes obscure from the moment we cut this grace away from the stream of life, which comes from the Father down to us and returns to the Father through the Holy Ghost in the Son.

For that is the personal, living way the Blessed Trinity dwells in us. We beg the reader's forbearance if we keep repeating the same words monotonously at every turn. The doctrine of grace, and of what is relevant to grace, has been so materialized, so "reified," that whenever a new problem comes to the fore we must remind the reader of the fact that these personal relationships of grace remain decisive for the solutions of *all* problems in the domain of grace.

The divine living presence in us signifies further that God speaks to us always anew in the concrete situations of our existence on earth. Our connections with God through grace never stiffen into abstract relations, much less into mechanical reactions. The ever-new—we feel tempted to say "alerting"—presence of God in our daily life is *God's providence*. Any situation we may have to face in the course of our earthly career, even sin, even *our own* sin, acquires in this light a meaning all its own. God speaks to us wherever we may be. Every situation is marked with its special duty and calling. God always holds the initiative in my life. As long as I live, I can never checkmate Him. He remains forever *faithful* to Himself. He pursues me in spite of my tepidness and my rebelliousness. And that is the drama (in the original Greek, *drama* means action), the dialogue between God and man. His invitation is ever renewed, always suited to the actual moment, and thus never an abstract plan that needs patching up each time something goes wrong with it. Looked at from that standpoint, the doctrine of God's primacy in grace keeps its unsurpassed, comforting significance unimpaired. In the third part of this book, we shall touch a last time upon the reality of divine providence in our lives.

What holds good in the life of the individual man is equally applicable to the history of a nation, or of the Church. Of course, our minds are as yet unfit to follow this polyphonic dialogue or even to form an idea of it for themselves. Before God, each one of us has his own name; but at the same time each remains a living member of one family, of one people, of the Church, of the immense human society. We have seen previously that God never severs these two real aspects of our existence from each other.

Predestination and History

Our preceding discussion has perhaps given an inkling of the way God guides man's life; He doesn't suppress it, but rather renews it and gives it greater depths. This personalistic mental outlook affords us at least a glimpse of the interior law, the inner dialectics of providence. Until now, however, an important aspect has escaped our notice. The Bible reveals to us that God is the Lord of history. He guides the nations where He pleases. One feels inclined to call it—though not very effectively—the externals of God's providence, the visible aspect of our history, such as the wars and disasters, the rise and fall of nations or civilizations.

But how God leads history we are unable to perceive. It is not even possible to point to an isolated fact as a "sign" of this divine guidance. Christ refused to adopt the Jewish notion that sickness, poverty or disaster overtaking a man in this life is necessarily a punishment for sin. Not even the decadence of a nation needs to be seen as a divine punishment of that nation. God's ways reach far deeper and wider. Our solidarity in both good and evil breaks across the boundaries of life, whether of an individual man or a family or a nation. Assuredly, sickness and all manner of evils are consequences of sin and should be thought of as punishment for sin. However, it has not been granted us to perceive the immediate connection between a given disaster and our sins. And so the ultimate sense of history escapes our perception. To unravel and discover its bearing, we should need to be God Himself.

Any recognition on our part of providence and the divine election at work in mankind takes place in the night of faith—a very dark night, indeed, for those who have no faith. We cannot pretend to experience the action of providence to any extent until love makes us realize that grace is life. Sin plunges man into total darkness; and for a man in darkness, the world is utterly senseless. All he can perceive are the troubling exterior appearances of things. That much has been conclusively established by the widely varying experiences different men had in concentration camps during the war. The camps had been transformed, with devilish ingenuity, into veritable hells. Some internees lost all faith, both in man and in themselves. Others, on the contrary, stumbled upon God for the first time in their lives in those surroundings from which, to all appearances, God had been banished. As I see things, it is along such lines that we can best appreciate the value of Father Aimé Duval's religious songs. He has appeared in our midst as troubadour of Christ's living presence in the slums, in the by-lanes, in the night, in sickness. We know, of course, that "God writes straight with crooked lines"; but unless we have the faith, we shall notice nothing more than the senseless scribblings of our human history.

At this point, the theologian too must keep silent. He knows, moreover, *why* he keeps silent: not from spiritual cowardice, nor from dull piety, but rather from a sense of awe. We must admit in all honesty that we have no real insight into God's ways. His activity transcends any and all activity within our experience. For God, time does not pass; youth is eternal; the freshness of the first day endures forever. Nor is there in Him any multiplicity of actions, one complementing another. He knows only of one action, reflected somehow in the checkered light and shade of the countless facets of our human history.

Grace means that God has always loved us. Through grace, He returns us to ourselves in liberal love. Such is our belief because He Himself has told us so, in Christ. But how He does it, we can only vaguely surmise.

What
May We

Part III

Expect
from Grace?

What should man expect from grace? The question sounds businesslike, perhaps rather cheering. We need to be cautious. Where God is involved, the question should not be what we can get but what God expects from us. The correction is not out of place, especially today when we witness a certain "humanizing" tendency in religious apologetics. Besides, who in his right senses dares ask from the one he loves, "What can I get from you?" A true lover seeks the good of the beloved, not his own gain. Grace is love. Though the above question is bound to raise objections, nonetheless we formulate it; after all we have said so far, it has a real, if secondary, meaning. Taking into account all that precedes, we are justified in examining the problem of the contribution of Revelation and theological thought to the general study of man. More precisely, perhaps, we may ask what grace changes in man. The reply is: nothing and everything. This final part undertakes to give nuance to such a bold answer.

Grace Changes Nothing

To begin with, we say that grace adds nothing to man's earthly nature and situation. Can we maintain this contention, and to what extent?

We said "nothing." For grace affects *directly and immediately* only the spiritual core of our person; it affects the rest insofar as it follows up the spiritual lines of force which emanate from that core and spread through the whole of our activity. Actual grace (as, for instance, in connection with good example, an inspiring book, etc.) opens the mind to divine things and awakens in the will a spiritual taste for them. But all the rest *remains what it was.*

There remains the world with its laws and its inevitable sequences of cause and effect. Storms and spring tides shatter the dikes on the coast, though baptized men and women are residing there. Cloudbursts cause rivers to break through their banks. Earthquakes lay waste whole cities. Historical laws continue to rule the destiny of nations, races and societies. Political mistakes must provoke reaction. Catholic states, parties or banks fare no better than others. It matters not a whit whether I am in a state of grace or not when my automobile hits a tree; the consequences are disastrous for the automobile, the tree and possibly the driver.

There remains also my body with its health, its illnesses, weaknesses and habits—and, unfortunately, its unmannerly tricks increasing with age. Grace has nothing in common with antibiotics. Each winter in this chilly country, I shall run up my usual score of colds. The surgeon who examines my case does not need to inquire whether I am in a state of grace; he may safely diagnose my condition and be satisfied that a resection of the stomach is necessary.

There remains further my psyche with its inborn or acquired urges, complexes and disturbances. Grace has nothing to do with leptosomes; it will not change my primary characteristics into secondary ones. The sacraments as such will cure neither neurasthenia nor schizophrenia; they leave a free hand to the psychiatrist, whether he advocates the method of Freud, Jung, Adler or the behaviorists.

There remain, too, my reasoning faculties and the peculiar nature of my will power, at least in their psychological and functional characteristics. Grace does not improve my memory or sharpen my wits or strengthen my volition—not directly, at any rate.

Why mention such obvious truths? Because these truths, so absurdly evident in the abstract, often lose their plainness when they affect us personally in the concrete. The time is past when professors at the Sorbonne in Paris could come out with *"Je n'ai jamais trouvé l'âme au bout de mon bistouri"* ("I have never found the soul under my scalpel") without even provoking a smile at their dreadful nonsense. But one still meets with scientists who fancy they can annex grace and the life of grace to the domain of their research, if only to deny their existence. Believing Christians, too, fail in logic when they hear of a fatal automobile accident and exclaim, "How is it possible! Such a good man!" Driving an automobile involves equal risks for all, good men or monsters.

As a first conclusion, we can hardly do better than hark back to the cautions set down in the first part of this book. Each science enjoys its own peculiar method. That method is conditioned by the specialized object of the science. We now add that it is of the utmost importance to remember that the specialized objects are not affected by grace either in their inner structure or in their functional relations. Consequently, the sciences remain undisturbed by the theology of grace as long as they keep to the investigation and ascertaining of fixed laws and relations among the *same specific phenomena*. One exception might be made here: philosophy takes up a privileged place as the "handmaiden" of theology—to use a metaphor, dear to the Middle Ages, for something that is no more than a half-truth. All the other sciences, as far as they move and operate within the limits of a clearly delineated field, need not worry about the question of grace; they enjoy an inalienable freedom of research and action within the framework of their speciality. This does not mean, however, that a man of science, as a human being and particularly as a Christian, has a right to remain indifferent to the reality of grace. For instance, a specialist will owe it to his faith not to fall prey to out-and-out materialistic hypotheses; his belief in grace will serve him as an alarm. But it will never interfere with matters belonging to his domain and method. We should add the remark that a surgeon would be an unworthy Christian if, before a dangerous operation, he showed serene indifference to the state of the patient's soul. His profession may indeed demand a great deal of discretion and objectivity, but never indifference to essentials.

Redemption Through the Incarnation

More remains to be said. We are coming to a second conclusion, the premises of which lie in deeper truth, and which will afford us fresh light on the full salvific significance of grace. We shall not satisfy ourselves with a ready-made, pedantic distinction between the downward trend of nature and the uplifting energy of grace. We have to dwell upon some theological aspects of redemption and grace, some points of considerable speculative and practical importance.

As we saw, grace and redemption are, more than anything else, God's creative, loving way of speaking to each one of us individually in Christ and in the Church. Now, the divine word does not find us located in the rarefied regions of a stratospheric spirituality where the trifling though very real cares and responsibilities of this puny world are lost to sight. God speaks to us *in the very concrete situation which is ours*. The essential message of redemption and grace is that we must surrender ourselves to God in faith, hope and charity here and now, on this earth, in the spot to which providence has consigned us and in which He wills us to dwell provisionally. As Roman Guardini wrote, it is planned by providence that God should speak to us really through the details of a determined situation. God is present in the daily events of our lives, calling us to His love. It is precisely this divine presence which gives our personal existence its deepest significance.

In God's design, our earth is entrusted with its own commission, a positive religious function. More will be said about this later. For the present, we should know that Revelation mentions another role our earth has to play, a

negative religious role: the role of "world," in the sense
frequently met with in Scripture, especially in St. John. The
world in this role means the realm of wickedness, the kingdom of the evil one, the place, too, of God's patience, the
historical space abandoned for a while to its own determina-
tion while the divine wrath bides its time in silence. Into
that world Christ came in order to save it. And in the midst
of that same world He planted His Church. Some of His followers may, in fact, belong to this world, though He Himself is "not of the world" (Jn. 17:14). However, taken in the
aggregate, they all have in common with and in Him an
inescapable task regarding this world of sin and evil. In
His sacerdotal prayer after the last supper, Christ addressed
His Father: "I pray not that thou shouldst take them out of
the world, but that thou shouldst keep them from evil. They
are not of the world, as I also am not of the world. . . . As
thou hast sent me into the world, I also have sent them
into the world" (Jn. 17:15-18).

The world, where sin and its consequences hold sway, is
thus the *place* where grace comes to us, where God speaks
to us of love and reconciliation, where, with the Son
and through the power of the Spirit, we return to the Father in faith and charity. We do so with and in Christ
because Christ Himself has done so. And here we meet with
the deepest significance of redemption.

Redemption denotes a divine gesture, one and perfect:
God's only begotten Son coming down into the world of
our perdition and thence returning to the Father, not alone
but with all those who share His Sonship through the divine
election and their own individual self-surrender. "I came
forth from the Father and came into the world. Again I
leave the world and go to the Father" (Jn. 16:28). The value
of the redemption is not to be measured by the sum of sufferings and humiliations undergone by Christ on the cross;
it is to be gauged by the perfect acceptance, from the
hands of the Father, of the situation Jesus freely assumed
in the world. His messianic appearance in the world could
not but cause a formidable avalanche of hatred, jealousy and
scandal. And Christ accepted it all for us, in our stead, but
also to teach us by His example how to act in like manner in
our respective callings. St. Paul brought out in a unique way
what the essense of redemption is when he wrote his celebrated text to the Philippians, a text which is still the basic
theme running through the pascal liturgy: "He humbled him-

self, becoming obedient unto death, even to the death of the cross" (Phil. 2:8). The cross is the culminating point, the supreme expression and therefore the highest visible symbol of Christ's obedience. Beyond dispute, the sum and substance of the redemption must be sought for in the love of the Messiah, the Son of God and the most beautiful of men, which caused Him to surrender Himself totally in humble obedience. Indeed, that was the only way to defeat sin; for sin, at bottom, is pride, rebellion and disobedience.

Christ's sanctity lay in His loving obedience to the Father. The grace He merited for us must consist in repeating, through life and till death, the Son's everlasting "Yes, Father," in loving obedience and surrender.

Grace in This World

As it was with Christ, so it is with us. Our holiness, the call of grace, lies in an ever-growing, ever more complete and humble acceptance of our life. And in this we can never be level-headed or businesslike enough. It is this life on this earth which is in question, this actual situation, here and now. The cross which we as Christians have to carry daily consists of our ailments, our failures, our discouragements, our sufferings, our weaknesses, our shame, our loneliness—all borne in humble obedience, like, with and in Christ.

Here again, but from a higher religious standpoint, we perceive that grace does not alter, remove or mitigate the consequences of sin on this earth—not directly, at least. The world will remain what it always was: the place where God is silently patient, and for us, a place of exile. Grace in this life attacks sin in its marrow of pride and disobedience. All the rest stays. The seed of sin is to be destroyed on the exact spot where sin strikes its root: in our fundamental personal option, in our deep-seated, proud rebellion against God. St. Augustine had this all-important issue of our lives in mind when he wrote, "Two societies have issued from two kinds of love: . . . selfish love which dared to despise even God, . . . love of God that is ready to trample upon self" (*De Civitate Dei*, 14:28). We are now able to grasp the sense of "self-contempt." The self to trample on is the self inasmuch as it is in league with the world, as it takes sides with sin and evil and goes against God.

At this point in our considerations, we may mention one or another exceptional occurrence. Grace sometimes erupts palpably into our impious world when God works miracles or grants our petitions. Looking at miracles with the eyes of simple religious faith, we understand that they merely confirm the general rule laid down in the preceding paragraphs. For miracles and, to a lesser degree, special instances of heard prayer are given no meaning by God other than that of being signs of the divine presence and thus also signs of divine grace.

Of their nature, miracles are not so exceptional as we tend to believe. Let us recall that, in spite of His silence, God is ever present in the world and speaks to us of His love in the intimacy of our hearts; further, from the religious standpoint, God's mysterious providence has no other purpose than to "stand by" us in whatever situation we may have landed in. Miracles and answers to prayer stand out as highlights of God's loving presence in our history. Far above the somber, low-banked clouds of sin, God's presence shines pure and glowing; in a miracle, the divine radiance breaks through.

In other words, to the eyes of faith the world remains always open to and charged with divine power. In the event of a miracle, this becomes momentarily perceptible in a divine sign.

On occasion the Father breaks His patient silence and discreetly drops His children the hint that He is there. Those delicate, unobtrusive signs of consolation, fidelity and love have the sole aim of stimulating us in the performance of our ordinary task. No other task has been entrusted to us than that of accepting this life just as it is, in humble, obedient love, holding fast to the one irreplaceable mainstay, which is faith in Jesus Christ, Who is the personal manifestation and presence of God in this world of sin and evil. His Church will endure till the end of time as His sanctuary, His tabernacle of the covenant, the visible pledge of His love. The other tokens God gave to mankind in the past become intelligible and are guaranteed in the light of God's manifesting Himself in the incarnation; all are evidence that God is discreet, even when testing us by His "obscurities." Like a soft halo, they enshrine the one radiant, tremendous event on earth: Christ's rising by His own power from the dead and becoming the "Lord," God in our midst.

Pessimism?

Some readers who have followed us this far may have gathered the impression that the role assigned to grace here on earth cannot fail to lead to fatalism or pessimism. But let me be well understood. From Revelation we do indeed learn that the true purpose of redemption is to bring us to accept fully the divine will regarding our concrete situation here below. This is far from suggesting fatalism of any kind, not even the kind prevailing in Islam; for it is God's will also that we do all we can to make the sufferings and disorders of this world as bearable as possible, both for ourselves and for our neighbors. A true son of the Church knows, as Christ did, that until redemption reaches its full perfection on the last day, he dwells in a world where vanity, egoism, the brutal will to power and pride will always endeavor to undo all medical, social, economic, technical and psychological progress. Did not a pagan say of old, *"Quid sunt leges sine moribus?"* ("What are laws without morality?")? No reform devised by human brain, *a fortiori* no dangerous mirage of an absolutely certain and irresistible human progress, can save man from the world where evil holds sway. The grace of Christ Jesus alone can do so by persuading us to follow in the Lord's footsteps, practicing humble obedience in faith and charity. God's Kingdom is not of this earth.

The Church, too, lives in exile in this world. It is a common weakness of ours to give way to the daydream that the Church, or at least some Christian social and political reforms, could definitely establish God's Kingdom in this world. The Middle Ages were haunted with this illusion, which we still have great trouble with today.

Conclusion

Let us sum up what precedes. On the one hand, grace does not abolish the regular natural functioning, the structures and interrelations of this created world. On the other hand, during the interval separating Christ's resurrection and ascension from His return in glory on the last day, the divine power of grace attacks the roots of sin in every free person. In the sinner, and notably in the one who deliberately shuts out God, sin with all its evil consequences is in the ascendant. But the man in the state of grace is *in* the world though not *of* the world, as our Lord Himself says. Redemption and grace enable us to accept in humble obedience, like and with Christ, the concrete situation allotted to each one on earth by providence; this is the way to engage in a head-on conflict with sin, to overcome sin and destroy it in its essence. This is also the way to meet and possess God.

Everything Is Grace

But faith tells us that besides its somber aspect, life also has its bright side. The complete Christian picture of life has always eluded colorless, oversimplified formulas. The human mind is so very limited, its conceptions are so unavoidably infirm that they often lead to heresy and sectarianism. God and the divine exceed all formulas. And so, in spite of a legitimate dose of pessimism, the true Christian should be radiant with an all-pervading optimism.

Grace gives us everything This is the last point we want to consider.

The Positive Religious Value of the World

First, let us give a corrective as a pendant to the preceding considerations. The universe in which we live also displays a positive religious aspect, and this, too, for and through Christ. By the mere fact that Christ entered into this world, the All-Holy into the realm of sin, His humanity has affected the world to its very foundations. Because He was not only man but also God, the world has found in Him a new center, a new basic principle and unifying law.

In Christ's humanity and body, the material world as a whole has been blessed; in germ it has been freed from its curse and once again oriented Godward. That is why, from now on, nature and this earth are fit to serve as signs and instruments of God's grace in a rich symbolism, archetypes of which lie hidden for the most part in the human psyche. The sacraments especially are evidence of this; so also to a lesser extent is the Church's liturgy. Ambivalently and by way of suggestion, the rites and symbols of other religions bear the same witness.

There is more. God has decreed that redemption and thus grace should come to man through the cooperation of other men. As we are mutually dependent on each other in regard to good and evil, Christ's great mercy has willed that no man should be saved without the cooperation of other men. To put it differently, we can and must work out with Christ the salvation of the world. It does not follow, though, that in this cooperation—or in any other capacity—we take up our stand next to Christ as His equals, as associates on a par with Him. Etymologically, the term *cooperation* here is too crude. We are allowed to work *with* Christ for the salvation of the world as far as we let ourselves be borne along and used by the one Savior to bring all men to Him, and inasmuch as Christ's life and action in our lives radiate His influence on our neighbors.

Every man, on receiving grace, has this duty imposed upon him. And this holds true for him who would receive grace outside the visible Church. But in the ultimate purpose and meaning of the Mystical Body, it is the prerogative of the Church, as the Body of Christ the head, to be the carrier and executor of His will and operation. In that light one may say that no grace, not even the most intimately personal one, is granted to the individual for himself alone; it must redound to the progress of the apostolate and to the general good of the Church.

Christian Optimism

Since through the incarnation all things have become instruments of Christ's almighty power, we are in duty bound to press into service anything that is good or useful to make Christ known. Grace and human nature are two widely different realities: grace belongs properly to the divine order, human nature does not. The latter should not be neglected on that account. Culture, humanism, civilization, adequate welfare, corporal and psychic health, artistic refinement, alliances between nations, even science and technology—normally, all have their share in the call of contributing to the salvation of mankind.

All things are called to serve. First, they serve as a negative preparation for grace. The less a man is hampered in his worship of God, the better for him. Culture, science and refinement may differ in nature from grace; competently used, however, they clear away many obstacles that hinder the action of God's Spirit. Herein precisely lies their negative role. It stands to reason that people will not be ready to lend an attentive ear to the message of grace as long as they are weighed down by ceaseless worry over how they will secure their daily morsel of bread; in such conditions they cannot but grow stunted and brutalized. No doubt God sometimes works in surprising ways, but experience has taught the Church that such is not God's *usual* way. Cardinal Newman had this same thought in mind when he wrote that persecution, with its ensuing ghetto mentality, leaves such an impression on the Catholic masses that few among them escape from it immune. A certain degree of political and social freedom is necessary to create a climate favorable to grace. And that is why the Church has always actively promoted a civilizing uplift whenever her missionary work lay among primitive races. She was far from thinking that a new convert could not be a good Christian unless he was also a good Portuguese or a good Spaniard, as has been asserted by some writers; but she knows that poverty, slavery and barbarism are obstacles to the efflorescence of grace.

Though the purely human values are not—let us repeat—grace in essence, they possess a positive value all their own in God's salvific plan. Contrary to ignorance, barbarism and backwardness, they provide signs and symbols of God's eternal glory. History shows that the Church has always considered it a divine mandate to foster science and culture, even when she had to face the task alone; her architecture and her liturgy are there to prove it. The Church firmly believes that in the beauty of nature and art and in the truth of science lie hidden the marvels of God's own beauty and wisdom. Should we ask for an unquestionable charter for Christian humanism, we have only to turn to the Epistle to the Philippians. Paul spoke first of the grace, the joy and peace caused by Christ's living presence in our midst: "Rejoice in the Lord always; again I say, rejoice. Let your forbearance be known to all men. The Lord is nigh! . . . and the peace of the Lord, which surpasseth all understanding, keep your hearts and mind in Christ Jesus." The Apostle then continued, "For all the rest, brethren, whatsoever things are true, whatsoever venerable, whatsoever just, whatsoever pure, whatsoever lovely, whatsoever commendable, if there be any virtue and if anything is praiseworthy, think on these things" (Phil. 4:4-8).

The World, a Life's Task

It is possible to proceed still farther in the consideration of the world's positive value. The world is God's gift. Every divine gift imposes an obligation because it is conferred on a free person. The world, it is true, has been singularly damaged by sin and robbed of its original purpose; but rampant evil cannot alter the fact that the world remains a gift, a workshop to serve as both room and instrument for culture and knowledge.

This last remark enables us to round off our argument. When we grant that a life of grace is simply a life of obedience on the very spot where God has placed us and where His grace and calling reach us, it follows that our earthly task of civilizing and mastering the universe falls within the wide scope of that very same obedience. For those who are servants of God and brothers of Christ in and through grace, the world with all it contains recovers its primordial meaning. And so grace means really everything to the baptized Christian. Whether good or evil, all things turn through grace into a definite duty and task. Paul said as much when he enlarged on the glories of the spirit and of grace, adding, "We know that to them who love God, all things work together unto good, to such as, according to his purpose, are called to be saints" (Rom. 8:28)—a text which might be interpreted: we know for certain that God directs all things to secure the good of those who love Him, those whom He has called for the fulfillment of His designs.

Christian humanism, then, is not entrusted only with the negative role of clearing external obstacles out of the way of grace, or the task of merely serving the Church in her apostolate. It should take pride in the profound *positive and religious* vocation received in and through grace. God's word makes the world transparent, turns it into a shrine and tabernacle of the divine, living presence. More still, all goodness, truth, virtue and beauty concealed in the world have been given to us in commission. Our humble obedience to grace, which is the secret of our salvation, demands that we take it all in hand, use it, cause it to bloom. A Catholic doctor finds in his faith a deeper, more convincing motive for a competent practice of his profession; so also the poet, the engineer, the social worker, any laborer or farmer. To put it in other words, our earthly career does not lie *outside* our Christian calling but on the contrary, well *within* it. Or more correctly still, our fundamental self-surrender to God in faith and charity has to find expression in the concrete details of our earthly career and dedication. On this level, too, we are God's fellow workers. The world is to us a *divine milieu* in which our earthly life achieves its fullest meaning, thanks to God's love.

These thoughts offer us the welcome opportunity of quoting a text of Ruysbroeck, often alluded to on previous occasions. The quotation shows how all the views set forth so far are brought together into one sober, genuinely religious vision of the world: "You know well that a meeting is a gathering of two persons coming from different places which in themselves are opposite and apart. Now, Christ comes from above as a lord and generous donor who can do all things. We come from below [from earth] as poor folk, devoid of strength and in need of everything. Christ comes in us from within outwards, and we come to Him from outside inwards. And for this reason, a spiritual meeting must here take place." [1] The words "we come from outside inwards" are now very telling. Beyond but through our *exterior* deeds of obedience, occupation and dedication, we tend to Christ *interiorly*. Here as always, especially in the supernatural order, we humans are concerned with the interiorizing process. Our scattered, insignificant daily actions should lead us, deep down in our hearts, to the great surrender in faith and love from outside inwards.

[1] Jan van Ruysbroeck, *Die Gheestelike Brulocht,* tr. Eric Colledge as *The Spiritual Espousals* (London: Faber & Faber, 1952), p. 143; see also p. 92.

Divine Grace and Matter

So far we have emphasized rather strongly how sharply grace is divided from the world. We accepted the term *world* in its twofold meaning: first, the meaning of space and "stage" for our human activity, and second, the meaning of kingdom of the evil one. This emphasis was necessary mainly in reaction against a lowering, ultimately pagan humanism which bypasses the exalted, unique nobility of a life of grace. But all reactions in the field of thought suffer fatally from onesidedness. Accents are shifted to the extent of falsifying the picture as a whole or of blotting out the correct accents. That was the way with heresy in the past.

When dealing with what is peculiar to grace, one is apt to strain after orthodoxy to the point of not doing justice to the wealth of God's Revelation. In the mind of the Greek Fathers, there existed no doubt whatever that the sacraments acted also on man's body. With apparent unconcern, they looked upon grace in terms of our bodily substance: grace meant immortality and everlastingness. This is all the more remarkable because the Greek Fathers were the great exponents of the transcendence of grace; grace was for them a divinization (*theopoiesis*), just as for Irenaeus the eucharist was the food and drink of immortality. It is probable that those Fathers were indebted for their manner of expression to some of their contemporaries, disciples of Plato and Plotinus, two philosophers who ruthlessly differentiated what (to their mind) is divine in the spirit from what is sinful in matter; but the essential of their faith they drew from other sources: they found it in Holy Scripture.

The Semitic mind embodied in Scripture (even in the Greek portion of the New Testament) sees no clear-cut distinction in man between spirit and matter. Flesh (*sarx*), soul (*psyche*) and spirit (*pneuma*) are three nouns standing for *the whole man* in his totality; they mean man seen now in his religious helplessness as creature, then in his sinning weakness or steeped in a sinful state of estrangement from God, or finally filled with the Spirit of God, the *Pneuma par excellence*.

The modern mind has recaptured something of this sense of totality. We have already pointed out that we are not souls tied to foreign bodies. As man, each one of us is but one unit, always itself, though in two manners of being which conflict with each other. We are wholly spirit and person, but have spiritual, autonomous self-possession. We are wholly matter, but have a being that grows and expands in time and space. We have here not two substances, rather unhappily stuck together, but two poles, two sources of energy, one subordinate to the other. That is why it is more exact to speak of two elements of one complex spiritual being which is confined to time and space but of which the spiritual element, aided by grace, holds the primacy.

Earlier in this book we stressed the fact that grace affects only our innermost spiritual core, permeating it and raising it. Along the same line of thought, we have shown that the miracles are the manifestation of the divine presence in a world that has emptied itself of God. These statements must stand. But in order that they not become onesided and false, the other aspect must be kept in mind as well: that man, even under the influence of grace, remains a single organic whole.

Maintaining all we have said before, we now assert that grace affects our being also in its material aspect, already here on earth. Both our body and the entire cosmos (which do not have to be thought of as divided from each other) receive a true germ of immortality, everlastingness and resurrection, in virtue first of Christ's redemption and second of our own personal grace of reconciliation. Our whole cosmic existence is necessarily involved in the reality of our rebirth in Christ. At the risk of dangerous misunderstandings and exaggerations on the part of literal-minded readers, we shall make bold to say that the sacraments, too, have their significance for cures of the body. The danger we allude to is not an imaginary one. We find evidence of it in some theologians who teach that the first and principal fruit of extreme unction is the physical healing of the sick. It is not hard to see what vain and false anticipation such unqualified statements are likely to raise in the mind of the average Catholic; but they nonetheless contain some elements of truth.

In the same order of thought, we could prove positively that miracles, seen in all their implications, convey to man a foretaste, a pledge and anticipation of the final cure and resurrection. They are more than mere symbols of Christ's victory over sickness, suffering and death; they are pregnant symbols, containing in germ what they witness to and signify.

Neither our body nor the cosmos as a whole remains un-affected by the mighty upheaval God's love causes in the si-lent secrecy of the heart. And in this sense, we are justified in asserting that grace means everything in life. From now on, we have the pledge of our resurrection; or better, we are risen already, seminally. We possess within us the seed of everlasting life, the remedy for all sickness, pain and death. What are infirmities, grief and dying if not sin made visible and tangible in this world? Besides, it is fitting that from now on the triumphant Lord should conquer the count-less manifestations of sin rampant in the world. But let us repeat once more: all this does not alter the fact that we are living in a world of sin and evil, of sickness and death, and that it is in this world that we have to find God in and through His first love.

Grace and Psychology

Something more has to be said. A great deal of attention is focused today on man's psychology, his nature and way of life. The question arises, does grace exercise any in-fluence on man's psychology?

It has already been pointed out that in the present order grace leaves man's psychology fundamentally unaltered. But thus set down, our words run the risk of oversimplifying matters. It bears repeating that psychic health and balance are in themselves quite different from grace, though on this point we have made some important corrective qualifications. To some extent we can acquire or improve them or redress them after one or another disturbance; we can in part main-tain them by human methods, sometimes by medicaments or even surgery. But grace is exclusively God's gratuitous gift in Christ. Further, the life of grace is made known to us only through faith. This is precisely why we drew atten-tion a few pages back to the fact that grace is also granted to those who are burdened with a psychosis or are sorely tried in their psychic equilibrium. Should such men, always with the help of grace, surrender themselves to God in the depth of their souls, they could actually reach a high state of sanctity, though their lives would perhaps not be of the kind of perfection which the Church likes to guarantee by a solemn canonization.

The purpose of canonization is largely conditioned by the requirements of the Church's history on earth. Canonizations, to be sure, remind the faithful of heaven. But when the Church canonizes, she intends primarily to propose to the piety and imitation of the faithful those followers of Christ whom divine providence has raised up to be models of a virtuous Christian life. The providential design of raising canonized saints in the Church according to the needs of the times has been dwelt upon by many writers in recent years. Now, in the case of persons undeniably privileged by grace but psychologically disordered through no fault of their own, spiritual oddities or morbid character traits would prevent them from being held up as models for imitation in the Church. Nonetheless, psychological disturbances are not necessarily obstacles to grace. God's ways are wonderful: He may, when He wants, destine some distraught souls to the sublime but harrowing vocation of imitating Christ forsaken and desolate in the Garden of Gethsemani, and this in spite of, or rather by means of, their shattered psychic condition. The essential requirement for holiness is the same for all: a faithful "yes" to the call of God, manifest in the particular concrete situation of existence which His wisdom has chosen for each one. The case of the psychotic is no exception to the rule.

From the moment such a man has made his fundamental surrender to God, he will tend to express it and live up to it in his daily actions; like any other human being, he has no other option. In him, however, the expression, execution and consciousness of this surrender to grace will be heavily handicapped, muddled up and traversed by psychic anxieties and disturbances. He may be tried by endless scruples; he may live under the permanent sway of a dark interior depression; he may forever relapse into aggressive fits of temper. But though he may suffer from any form of psychic disease, he is in no way prevented from accepting himself from God's hand as he is, with the right dispositions of whole-hearted humility and self-abasement. Though he may be hovering on the brink of insanity, in moments of lucidity he can still answer the merciful voice of God, throw himself in His arms and moan with the psalmist, "Out of the depth I have cried to thee, O Lord" (Ps. 129:1). In his own depressed and anxious manner, he can exclaim with and in Christ, "Father, into thy hands I commend my spirit" (Lk. 24:26). Such cases do occur; they belong to history; but unfortunately they are not generally known.

However, such is not the normal way of grace. To quote Ruysbroeck for the last time, Christ comes in us "from within outwards." God's grace transforms, heals and raises our fundamental option. The normal way with God's saving action is that an efficacious virtue flows from this interior rebirth of the heart, and little by little permeates, strengthens, unifies and enkindles human activity as a whole. In the ordinary designs of divine love, the process of interior unification in God brings about a behavior authentically human, a perfect psychic integration. The divine action of grace promotes an interior harmony of all our powers, aspirations and impulses, not only in order to purify them but also to give them deeper root and greater intensity. God works "from within outwards." Grace radiates outward when it is given free scope in our life.

Grace brings with it peace and joy, even in the midst of pain, trials and desolation, because it attaches and directs the heart to God. That peace and that joy do not well up from a mundane source, but they prolong themselves and re-echo in the human psyche. Increasing attention is given today in psychology and psychiatry to the energy and balance generated by interior repose, by contentment with self and others, by joy and above all by esteem and love. Nothing enriches or fulfills human life so much as the genuine respect and affection of others; they act potently upon the human psyche, and contribute to our bodily functions and general health. The Christian is indebted to faith for a deeper insight into his sinfulness, but he also owes to it a blissful awareness of the Father's unique love in Christ for his lowliness and impotence. No one can fail to see that faith purifies, unifies and even strengthens on the merely human level—the *normal* outcome of a living, supernatural faith.

Few people seem to realize and acknowledge this after-effect, because too many deliberately refuse to cooperate with grace. Within that class must be reckoned a number of persons specially consecrated to God. Victims of neurasthenia and moral depression are met with in religious houses. The causes are not always the same. In the case of cloistered communities, the blame lies sometimes with the neglect of elementary laws of corporal and psychological hygiene on the part of the superiors; these are often appointed to leadership more on account of their overwrought piety than because of their knowledge of men. And that cannot be helped. However, the source of mental upsets, with far worse consequences, must be sought on a deeper level. They are to be traced back to infidelity to grace, shown perhaps in the spiritual mediocrity with which the divine call is lived up to.

Let a man give himself to God entirely and definitively, and without ceasing to be a limited onesided human being, and he will take up his stand on another level: the level of the saints. All the lives of the saints are enchanting, unique, arresting. Blinkered, moralizing hagiographers do their best to portray them all in the same drab colors, stripped of all originality. But a look at the actual facts of their histories is enough to convince us that originality and intensity of life are nowhere so finely displayed as in the world of the saints. Each one of them, borne along by grace, was surprisingly faithful to the bent of his own particular temperament and character, as given to him by providence. The wellspring of originality lies hidden in each one's fundamental liberty. And because grace heals and raises just that fundamental liberty, the world of the saints cannot but be fascinating.

Scripture teaches the same lesson. Whatever some moralizing preachers may say, Holy Scripture, especially the Epistles, insists on the fact that Christ's grace in us must shine as a *witness and revelation* of God's glory. "So let your light shine before men, that they may see your good works, and glorify your Father who is in heaven" (Mt. 5:16). Nowhere do we find attention so frequently called to the high duty of *rejoicing* in the risen, redeeming Christ. Christian joy is our principal testimony. The Church has traversed periods of such ruthless persecution that joy remained the one way in which the Christian could bear witness to his faith, though harassed and sent to death. Georges Bernanos makes his Carmelite nuns sing throughout the night preceding their trial in prison, and after the trial, up to the very steps of the guillotine. In this, history bears him out. Grace is indeed all-important to us, even from the point of view of human psychology.

How could it be otherwise? To a lover everything shines

with love. Shadows vanish and light illumines all things. Sickness, care and failure become trifling, easy to bear. If this is so with human love, what must it be in the case of a man filled with the love of God? Gone are the conventions of a routine Catholic life that has locked itself up and stiffened into lifeless, set formulas and practices. Can true religion be lived in a rut? The question answers itself.

Conclusion

We shall be short. Catholicism is without illusions; it is level-headed and realistic—like God, Who sees all things and judges all things in the light of truth. The Catholic outlook on life, based on the theology of grace and redemption, is probably a great deal more pessimistic than that of some pagans of antiquity; it is also more somber than what modern pagans advertise today as enlightened wisdom. Basic in our faith is the knowledge that we dwell in a world of sin, that we are affected by it in the core of our being and that the absolute heinousness of sin is to be discovered only in the shadow of the cross. No one can show himself naively optimistic, though here and there we meet Christians who play up to the mood of their contemporaries by sweetening our pessimism with their own brand of humanism, which keeps too little of Christ's teaching.

But precisely because we are pessimistic over man and the world we can afford to be intensely optimistic and happy.

In the course of this book, we have made good use of Chapter 8 of the Epistle to the Romans, in which Paul summed up in a masterly way what he held on the subject of divine grace. It is typical of the man to have concluded that chapter with the lines which we now quote.

What else can we add to all this? If God is on our side, who can be against us? He did not even spare his own Son, but gave him up for us all. How then would he not freely give us all things along with him? Where is the man who can bring any charges against the elect whom God has justified [and thus freed and saved]? Where is the man who will pass sentence against us, when Jesus Christ, who died, nay, rose again, and sits at the right hand of God, is pleading for us? Who will separate us from the love of Christ? Will affliction, or hardship, or persecution, or hunger, or nakedness, or danger, or the sword? . . . But in all these circumstances we are conquerors, through him who granted us his love. Of this I am fully persuaded [and for us, too, this ought to become a certainty and a consolation]: neither death, nor life, nor angels and principalities, nor powers [in the heavens, according to Jewish notions in Paul's time], neither what is present, nor what is to come, nor any force whatever, neither the height above us, nor the depth beneath us [all of which are supposed sources of opposition which serve to enlarge in concrete terms on the word *nothing*], nor any other creature, will be able to separate us from the love of God which comes to us in Christ Jesus our Lord. [Rom. 8:31-39]

Our life of grace is so deeply rooted in Christ that our triumph in and with Him is assured already here below. "Have confidence, I have overcome the world" (Jn. 16:33): these words, taken from the farewell speech of Jesus to His disciples, are a lasting treasure for all of us to carry in our hearts. The conscious remembrance of them will cause happiness and joy to grow in a steady crescendo. We are saved. To the saved in grace and love, everything existing takes on a new look. In everything, everywhere and always, we recognize the features of Christ—"the bleeding head so wounded" no less than the glorified face on Tabor and on Easter morning. "This is the day which the Lord has made. Let us be glad and rejoice therein."

Other MENTOR-OMEGA Books

THE LOVE OF LEARNING AND THE DESIRE FOR GOD: A Study of Monastic Culture by Jean Leclercq, O.S.B.

An examination of the manuscripts of the medieval monasteries reveals their role in preserving the culture of the past. By a distinguished scholar and Benedictine monk.
(#MT432—75¢)

A PREFACE TO METAPHYSICS   by Jacques Maritain

An introduction to the science of metaphysics in seven brilliant lectures by the distinguished French Neo-Thomist. (#MP403—60¢)

ELEMENTS OF CHRISTIAN PHILOSOPHY
by Etienne Gilson

The noted French philosopher illuminates the key ideas of the theology of St. Thomas Aquinas.
(#MT489—75¢)

PSYCHOANALYSIS & PERSONALITY   by Joseph Nuttin

The noted Belgian psychologist discusses the relation between modern depth psychology and Christian philosophy. Newly revised edition. (MT426—75¢)

LEISURE: THE BASIS OF CULTURE   by Josef Pieper

A penetrating indictment of the 20th century cult of work and hectic amusements, which can ultimately destroy both our culture and ourselves. Introduction by T. S. Eliot.
(#MP550—60¢)

THE DEAD SEA SCROLLS AND PRIMITIVE CHRISTI- ANITY   by Jean Danielou

A Jesuit Professor at the Catholic Institute of Paris demonstrates the relationship between the facts revealed in the ancient scrolls and the traditional view of Christian faith. (#MP405—60¢)

THE DYNAMICS OF WORLD HISTORY
by Christopher Dawson

A renowned historian examines the relation between religion and civilization, and shows Christianity as the central, dynamic force in man's historical progression.
(#MQ378—95¢)

TO OUR READERS: If your dealer does not have the SIGNET and MENTOR books you want, you may order them by mail, enclosing the list price plus 10¢ a copy to cover mailing. If you would like our free catalog, please request it by postcard. The New American Library of World Literature, Inc., P. O. Box 2310, Grand Central Station, New York, New York, 10017.